GROWING
roses
FOR SMALL GARDENS

The Christopher Helm 'Growing' series also includes:

Growing Begonias
Eric Catterall

Growing Bromeliads
Barry Williams and Ian Hodgson

Growing Bulbs
Martyn Rix

Growing Chrysanthemums
Harry Randall and Alan Wren

Growing Cyclamen
Gay Nightingale

Growing Dahlias
Philip Damp

Growing Fuschias
K. Jennings and V. Miller

Growing Gladioli
Ron Park and Eric Anderton

Growing Irises
G. F. Cassidy and S. Linnegar

GROWING
roses
FOR SMALL GARDENS

Michael Gibson

CHRISTOPHER HELM
A & C Black · London

TIMBER PRESS
Portland, Oregon

© 1990 Michael Gibson

Line illustrations by David Henderson

First published 1990 by Christopher Helm
(Publishers) Ltd, Imperial House,
21–25 North Street, Bromley, Kent BR1 1SD,
a subsidiary of A & C Black (Publishers) Ltd,
35 Bedford Row, London WC1R 4JH

ISBN 0 7136-8030-X

A CIP catalogue record for this book is
available from the British Library.

First published in North America in 1990 by
Timber Press
9999 S.W. Wilshire
Portland, Oregon, 97225

ISBN 0-88192-186-6

Phototypesetting by Florencetype Ltd,
Kewstoke, Avon
Reproduced, printed and bound in Great
Britain by Biddles Ltd, Guildford

CONTENTS

Colour Plates

FIGURES

CHAPTER 1

WHY SMALL ROSES?

In 1864 that prolific gardening writer of his day, Shirley Hibberd, could say in his *The Rose Book* without sounding particularly ridiculous: 'Fifty in a batch may look fine, but ten clumps of five each may have a very paltry appearance unless the Rosarium is on so small a scale as to be beyond the reach of criticism.'

Nowadays he would not find much to write about that was worthy of his rather grandiloquent pen, for we garden on a very different scale. We are all—or nearly all, for we must not forget the gardeners of The National Trust and their like — 'beyond the reach of criticism', but it is just as important to make a success of a small space as a large one and can sometimes be more difficult. That is the reason for this book, to try to point the way to dealing with the kind of garden we see about us every day, the kind that most of us possess.

Gardens of whatever size need plants which are in scale with them and really big areas tend to be broken up into smaller units in recognition of this, for the majority of plants are quite small. A big garden could accommodate a 3 × 2.4m (10 × 8ft) *Rosa soulieana* but a patio probably could not. A lakeside could accommodate a gunnera, but a small goldfish pond could not, which emphasises the point I am making, but it might be thought that the average rose—the Hybrid Tea or Floribunda—is not really all that big. Will it not fit perfectly well into the garden of today? Quite true. It will, and some space will be given to the uses of a small selection of them, but the main emphasis of this book will be on the marvellous and constantly expanding range of new roses which has come into existence in the last few years and many of which are specifically intended for small-scale plantings. They open up all sorts of possibilities that could never have been contemplated in Shirley Hibberd's day.

First there are the dwarf cluster flowered or patio roses, which are mostly very low-growing versions of the kind we have known for many years as Floribundas, and secondly there are shrub roses. For far too long people have been saying that shrub roses are too large for a small garden, and in the case of species and a good many of the others this has been to

1 Outline of a typical small old garden rose

2 Outline of a typical patio rose

3 Outline of a typical small modern shrub rose

some extent true. But not completely, for there have always been small shrub roses for those who were prepared to delve a little into nursery catalogues to find them. It has also been said, and this is a much more valid objection, that all the older shrub roses only flower at midsummer, and one has to consider whether or not a non-remontant rose is good value in a small garden when one that flowers right through into the

2

autumn could be used instead. In a large area a once-flowering rose can be forgotten when other things take its place as the season changes. In a small garden there may not be room for other things.

There are, however, people who love the old shrub roses and would not want to be without at least one or two of them on whatever scale they garden, so some have been included. However, once again the emphasis is on the modern and particularly on a new race of shrub roses which have been specially bred for modern gardening conditions and are mostly remontant into the bargain.

Some years ago, ground cover plants became fashionable. People were tired of weeding and were looking for something that would smother weeds and at the same time look decorative. Rose breeders, sensing the trend, decided to try to produce what they were looking for and the result, only now emerging for new roses cannot be produced overnight, is a wonderful range of shrub roses which are low-growing and tend to spread out sideways rather than upwards. Many will not exceed 1m (3ft) in height or spread out much more than that all round, and what could be better for a small garden?

The uses of miniature roses in a small garden are self-evident. Less so, perhaps are the uses of climbing roses, where once again modern breeders have come up trumps. The sheer exuberance of many of the old kinds has been curbed and the climbers being produced nowadays are demure by comparison. Even a garden that was no more than a small paved yard could sport a climbing rose in a tub, provided always that there was something up which it could climb. There are few gardens that do not have a house attached, and houses have walls which, provided that they are not permanently in shade, are ideal for the training of a climbing rose. They take up very little ground space.

CHAPTER 2

PATIO ROSES

From what has been said in the last chapter, it will be realised that these small Floribundas should really be called dwarf cluster flowered roses, which I find hard to go along with. The new term 'cluster flowered' for Floribundas is already confusing enough when one considers how many other groups of roses have clusters of flowers (most of the shrub roses, for instance), and when the word dwarf is added it becomes not only confusing but has a touch of the grotesque. The word 'dwarf' is not one with which, however unjustly, one immediately associates delicate beauty, and I understand that The World Federation of Rose Societies, which decides these matters, is beginning to think again about some of the terminology it adopted in making a long-overdue and mostly worthy effort to sort out rose classification.

Not that the popular alternative name of 'patio roses' is ideal as it suggests a limitation of use. One might be excused for thinking that the roses could only be used on patios which is, of course, far from the case. If anyone can come up with a better alternative I know that the rose trade, and I am sure the general public too, would welcome it.

I have said that patio roses are small Floribundas but, depending on which way you look at it, one could also say that they were large miniature roses, for they have actually been developing from two directions at the same time. The world's breeders have realised at last that the small rose has a place of ever-increasing importance, as gardens shrink in size in tune with modern living, and so they have been concentrating on producing them. At the other end of the scale, the hybridisers of miniatures have, over a much longer period, used crosses with Floribundas to introduce new colours into their breeding lines with the result that, along with the new colours, has come an increase in size. At length the point has been reached when it is impossible to say to which class certain roses belong. The two groups have met in the middle and formed a new class, but nobody, as we have seen, has so far found a really satisfactory name for it. For convenience I will continue to refer to them as patio roses.

It is rather strange to think, however, that, whatever one calls them, they are in a sense a step backwards in time. In their size, their habit of growth, and in their uses in the garden, they much more closely resemble the old Polyantha roses than anything else, from which the small Floribundas, though not the miniatures, are directly descended.

So much of the early development of our garden roses took place in France that it is not surprising to learn that the story of the Polyantha, leading in turn to the story of the Floribunda and then the patio rose, starts there. Jean-Baptiste Guillot, a rose breeder and nurseryman of Lyons (who, incidentally, raised the first Hybrid Tea, 'La France', in 1867) started to experiment in the second half of the last century with a Japanese species rose called *R. polyantha*. It has since had its name changed to *R. multiflora*, but still makes the same large, tangled bush with shoots almost of rambler proportions and carrying at midsummer large clusters of small, white flowers. It is not revealed what M. Guillot crossed this rose with, but it was almost certainly one of the recently introduced China roses, which he hoped would pass on its remontant habit. In this he succeeded and in 1875 he put on the market the first of a completely new class of rose, the Polyantha. This was called 'Ma Paquerette' and was quite small, the result presumably of the restraining influence of the China rose on the exuberant *R. polyantha*, and it carried its flowers in large clusters.

The new class was developed rapidly, for the gardening public loved them, but it was not until the salmon-pink 'Orléans Rose' was introduced in 1909 that they really became established, with a popularity that was to last right up to the time of the 1939–45 war. Their peak probably came during the first quarter of this century, though they continued to be grown for a long time after that and a few of them are still in the lists of specialist growers.

They were short, bushy growers with, like 'Ma Paquerette', clusters of flowers, often globular in shape, but of a rather limited colour range. Many of them were very prone to mildew at a time when fungicide sprays were nothing like as effective as they are today, and they were extremely likely to produce sports. Several of the best-known varieties, like 'Coral Cluster' and 'Cameo', were sports of 'Orléans Rose' and this habit could be disconcerting if they were used for bedding. If a bed of one kind were planted a gardener could be excused for being annoyed if some bushes produced flowers of a different colour. This must also have made nurserymen nervous about stocking them in case they turned out to be quite unlike the rose their customers had ordered but, despite these considerable drawbacks, they continued to flourish and other hybridists began to use them in their breeding lines.

Joseph Pernet, another Lyons nurseryman and the same one who brought us our bright yellow bedding roses, tried crossing Polyanthas with the then popular large flowered Hybrid Perpetuals. In 1891 he came up with 'Mlle Bertha Ludi' the flowers of which were white with a carmine flush, which could reasonably be claimed as the first Floribunda. However, it was a long time before that name was to be adopted for a new class, and 'Mlle Bertha Ludi' had well and truly vanished from cultivation by the time that happened.

1907 brought 'Annchen Muller' from Schmidt in Germany, and in 1909 came one that has outlasted practically all of them. This was 'Gruss an Aachen', which is so much alive today that it is among the varieties recommended in this book.

Svend Poulsen, a Danish hybridist this time, was another who realised the potential of the Polyanthas for producing larger and healthier cluster flowered roses, and began to cross them with various Hybrid Teas. His first real success came in 1912 with 'Red Riding Hood' ('Rödhatter'), though it was to be another twelve years before he achieved commercial success with the arrival of 'Ellen Poulsen', followed by 'Kirsten Poulsen' later in the same year. These were the first roses really to resemble the Floribunda as we know it today, though they were actually known then as Hybrid Polyanthas. Unofficially, as so many of the varieties that followed came from the same breeder, among them 'Anne Poulsen' and 'Karen Poulsen', they were usually called Poulsen roses. Just the same there were notable varieties raised by others, two of the best being 'Donald Prior' and 'Betty Prior' from England.

All this did not mean that the Polyanthas themselves had been abandoned. There were notable sports from a rose called 'Echo', which had been introduced by Lambert of Germany in 1914. One of these sports was 'Greta Kluis', which appeared in 1916 and began a whole series of roses which sported one from the other, culminating in 'Anneka Koster' in 1927, pink 'Dick Koster' in 1929, and finally the orange-salmon 'Margo Koster'. The latter, though hardly remembered now in the United Kingdom, is still popular in America, both as a garden and as a pot plant.

'Echo' also appears in the lineage of the first rose actually to be called a Floribunda. Crossed with the Hybrid Tea 'Rev. F. Page-Roberts' in 1934, it resulted in a rose with clusters of small flowers, each with high-centred blooms like those of its Hybrid Tea parent. It was called 'Rochester' and was so unlike anything seen before that it was decided that a new class name was needed. Floribunda was decided on, though the name had no botanical validity, and it was some time before the powers that be both in America and in the United Kingdom were prepared to accept it. It was, in fact, late in the 1940s before the term Floribunda was recognised in England.

From about 1940 onwards a whole series of Floribundas from Edward Le Grice of Norfolk, among them pink 'Dainty Maid' and 'Bonnie Maid' and deep red 'Dusky Maiden', played a major part in increasing the popularity of this type of rose. However, unlike 'Rochester', most of these had single or semi-double flowers, which opened wide to reveal their stamens. This was a reversion to the Poulsen type of bloom; but in the late 1940s a dramatic change came from across the Atlantic. The breeder Eugene Boerner introduced his new semi-double and double-flowered Floribundas, almost all with high-centred flowers, at least when they were in the bud. These included 'Goldilocks', 'Masquerade', 'Fashion' and 'Spartan' which, in addition to re-introducing the Hybrid Tea flower form, brought new colours with them as well. 'Masquerade' was the sensation, actually changing its colour as it aged, not by fading, but by going from yellow, through pink to (it must be confessed) a rather dirty red, while 'Fashion' and 'Spartan' were both salmon-pink, which had not been seen in rose blooms before.

A search was now on for bigger blooms, though it was difficult to see the reasoning behind it. The only result was to produce roses with larger flowers and fewer in the truss, so that it became impossible at times to tell whether they were Floribundas or Hybrid Teas. Some of them were taller growers as well, and as a class these became known as Grandifloras in America. The UK, however, would have none of this and chose in its wisdom (if you could call it that) to call them Floribunda Hybrid Tea-Type. The most notable example of a Grandiflora, and the one that made people realise that a new class name was needed, was and is 'Queen Elizabeth'.

While some of the Floribunda ancestors of the patio rose were busy producing bigger and better varieties, developments were also taking place at the other end of the scale, though a good deal more slowly. For a long time there had been a few small Floribundas such as 'Tip Top', 'Topsi' and 'Marlena', in addition to roses in the Polyantha strain such as 'Yvonne Rabier', 'The Fairy' and 'Little White Pet'. They had been used by the discerning, but it is only in very recent years that the value of the small rose for the small garden has really been appreciated, with 'The Fairy' setting the pace. In this case demand probably came before supply. People decided they liked the small roses and the breeders and nurserymen responded—but new roses cannot be produced overnight. Now, though, they are rolling off the production lines at a phenomenal rate. And the choice is bewilderingly wide.

As has already been said, despite their name, patio roses can be used anywhere, the name being merely intended to give an indication of their size. However, they are small and so in the main are patios, and thus they suit each other particularly well. This makes their use on patios a good place to start discussing how best they can be utilised in the garden. First, however, to define a patio.

My dictionary describes it as 'An inner court open to the sky in a Spanish or Spanish American house' or, alternatively, 'An area, usually paved adjoining a house, used for outdoor living', which just about covers it, though there are a number of variations that have been successfully tried. A patio can be away from the house, perhaps in a spot where two garden walls meet to form a backing or screen, or beside a swimming pool with a trellis screen or perhaps a summerhouse or changing room helping to give the feeling of enclosure that is generally associated with patios. A patio normally seems to have a vertical element as well as a horizontal one.

If a patio is to be used regularly for outdoor living it is probably better situated close to the house. Outdoor living includes enjoying meals in the open air, and if the distance from the kitchen to the eating area is too great this can soon become a source of irritation. And chairs and tables may have to be carried in and out, which again suggests that it is more sensible if the patio can be reached easily, either from the house or from a shed where they are kept. Paving the patio is really essential in such a situation as it will dry out relatively quickly and there will be no mud to trample into the house.

Although the majority of patios are paved, this does not mean that gaps cannot be left, either for small, isolated beds in which a patio rose such as 'Bright Smile' or 'Boys' Brigade' can be grown in groups of three or even as single specimens, or perhaps a long bed right down one side of the patio with for example the small and very compact apricot-pink 'Sweet Dream'. The choice of rose will, of course, be up to you and you might even want to pick one that tones in with the covers of your chairs—provided that there is a reasonable chance of these remaining the same for a number of years!

If you decide to have a bed on the side of the patio nearest to the house, particular care will have to be taken to make sure that it is regularly watered. It is unlikely to be a very wide bed and it will probably not have a great deal of soil in it. The bricks of the wall will absorb much of the moisture, and should there be overhanging eaves as well the bed will end up very dry indeed. This will not suit the roses.

The same thing applies, though not to quite the same extent, if your patio is surrounded by low brick walls. If your beds run along these it is best to treat your roses almost as if they were growing in containers and water them accordingly.

Patio roses are the ideal plants for containers. Ordinary bush roses—Hybrid Teas and Floribundas—can, unless they are very carefully chosen, tend to look top-heavy. The most popular modern roses are not the most elegant of plants in shape or habit and, if it was not for the beauty of their flowers and in some cases their glossy leaves, they would not find a place in many gardens. Their sometimes rather leggy and gaunt habit tends to be cruelly exposed when they are grown in pots or other containers, whereas the bushy and mound-forming habit of so many of the patio roses and modern shrub varieties presents a very different picture. Provided that the container is of the right size and it is watered regularly they will be perfectly happy and, unless stone troughs have been used, they are comparatively easy to move around. This has obvious advantages and is much easier than lifting paving stones and replacing others if you wish to change your planting scheme. Never forget, however, whether you are making more or less permanent beds in the paving or else using containers, that both must be positioned in a place where the sun can reach them for a minimum of half the day. This is a consideration to bear in mind if you are proposing to site your patio on the north side of your house.

4 Patio roses can be grown in a tub, in a trough or in a gap left by the removal of one or more paving stones in a patio

As has already been indicated, the most important thing with containers for roses is that they should be large enough. They must be deep enough to give a good root-run, and even with the comparatively small patio roses it is as well to allow about 38cm (15in), and the container, be it wooden tub or a trough, should be large enough to allow the roots to spread out sideways. Free drainage is essential and so, even if there appear to be adequate drainage holes, it is as well to stand the container on bricks or blocks of some kind to make sure that the water can really get away freely. Plenty of broken crocks should go in the base of the container and a soil-based potting mixture such as John Innes No. 3 is suitable.

9

Commercial mixes can be expensive if your patio is a sizeable one and you are using a lot of large containers, so it might be practical to mix your own growing medium. This is best done a few weeks before planting is to begin, keeping it in a cool, dry shed, and turning it occasionally while it matures. A suitable recipe is good, turfy loam, well-moistened granulated peat and clean sharp sand in the ratio of 4:2:1. For each 10-litre (2-gallon) bucket of this, add 30g (1oz) each of hoof and horn meal and super-phosphate of lime, and 15g (½oz) each of bonemeal and potassium sulphate, all well mixed in.

Watering is, as has been said, very important, but it can in time leach the goodness from the soil. To overcome this a liquid rose fertiliser (keeping strictly to the instructions on the bottle when mixing it) can be added to the water about every two weeks during the growing season. Alternatively a slow-acting dry fertiliser can be worked gently into the surface soil with a handfork early in the year, to be followed by a thorough watering.

Although the roses on a patio may be receiving some protection from the elements, from surrounding or partially surrounding walls, this does not mean that they will be any less prone to the ills from which other roses suffer. If black spot or mildew appear they must be sprayed (though not during the course of a barbecue!), they must be dead-headed, and all the other tasks that rose growing involves must be carried out. The only exception to this is that, with the short-growing roses described in this book, they will not need cutting back in early autumn to prevent wind-rock.

Pruning of patio roses will have to be done in the spring, using the pattern for any short-growing Floribunda. This involves the removal of dead or diseased wood and weak, spindly shoots, and the thinning out of tangled growth if this is necessary. After this, bearing in mind some overall shaping of the bush, the remaining main shoots can be cut back to 10–13cm (4–5in) in length. More general details about pruning will be found in Chapter 7.

So much for patio roses on the patio. How can they be used in the remainder of a small garden?

Once more containers will be to the fore. A tub with a patio rose in it on either side of a door, or on short brick pillars at the head and foot of steps would be one way of using them. Another would be the placing of troughs planted with patio roses down each side of a porch, provided that the roof of the porch did not completely shelter them from the rain or keep the sun away. In addition, the path from the porch to the front gate will gain a new dimension and lighten one's step if it is lined with apricot-orange 'Clarissa' or salmon-pink 'Dainty Dinah'. Both, or almost any other you choose to name, would be pretty continuously in flower

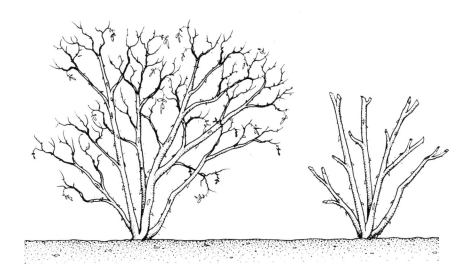

5 Pruning a patio rose

from late June until the frosts, and the comparatively long stems of 'Clarissa' would provide flowers for the house. Any path would look well when lined with patio roses, which have the advantage that, because of their small stature, their shoots do not become bowed down with rain so that they tip water into the shoes of a passer-by.

Patio roses are also ideal for edging beds of taller roses, or indeed of other plants, and are less inclined to be overawed by their neighbours as miniature roses can be when used for the same purpose. But it must always be remembered that they need their fair share of sun, and this must be taken into account in deciding what other plants they can be combined with. The north side of a border of tall-growing plants would not be a suitable spot.

In beds, patio roses can look very well planted in clumps of three or four. This kind of planting can be in beds set on their own in lawns, or the groups can be part of a mixed planting in a herbaceous border, in which case they should be reasonably near the front. However, herbaceous borders are not very common nowadays, especially in small gardens and need more dedication to their well-being than most people have the time or the inclination to give. This does not mean, of course, that one cannot have a mixed border with patio roses in it, but it will probably be on a less daunting scale.

If you are using patio roses purely for bedding on their own, it is probably best not to mix varieties if your space is limited to a dozen roses or less. A mixture can produce a rather patchy effect as not all varieties

11

reach their peak flowering period at the same time. The buds of one may be just opening while the flowers of another are fading, so that a carefully planned colour combination may be only partially effective. However, if the temptation to mix cannot be resisted, once more plant the roses in groups of three or four of each variety. A greater degree of flowering continuity will be achieved that way, or at any rate there will always be more colour showing at any one time.

Having suggested the addition of patio roses to beds containing other plants, one must next consider adding other plants to a bedding scheme predominantly of patio roses. The question of size will come into it more than with other roses and rather limits what can be used. It really comes down to shrubs used as a background or possibly an edging of traditional annual bedding plants such as white alyssum, ageratum or lobelia. Or an edging of something a little bigger and less usual might do, such as *Anaphalis triplinervis*, but on the whole I feel that edging plants for these small roses are both fussy and quite unnecessary.

Below, the first of our variety lists begins, showing a selection of the best of the patio roses. Many are very new, but some come from the quite distant past and have been more usually found under the heading of Polyantha. Most reach a height of between 45cm and 60cm (1½–2ft).

Varieties of patio rose

Baby Bio Smith, 1977. 'Golden Treasure' × seedling
Has clusters of bright yellow blooms, fairly large and full and with a slight scent. They are large for the size of the plant, which is compact and bushy, not exceeding 45cm (18in) in height.

Bashful De Ruiter, 1955. Parentage not given
One of a number of roses coming from the same raiser and named after the Seven Dwarfs in Walt Disney's *Snow White*. Small, single flowers in bright, reddish-pink and with a white eye. Carried in very large trusses on a short, bushy plant.

Bianco Cocker, 1983. 'Darling Flame' × 'Jack Frost'
One of the best of the miniature roses, crossed with the white Hybrid Tea, 'Jack Frost', produced this 38cm (15in), bushy, spreading rose with its enchanting, creamy-white, rosette-type flowers carried with great freedom.

Boys' Brigade Cocker, 1983. ('Dickson's Flame' × 'St Albans') × ('Little Flirt' × 'Marlena')
Neat and compact with large trusses of semi-double, red flowers that

have creamy-yellow centres. No scent but a striking and unusual rose that will catch everybody's eye.

Buttons Dickson, 1987. Parentage not given
Beautifully shaped buds open to elegant, salmon-red flowers on well-spaced sprays. A neat, bushy grower which will reach about 45cm (18in) in height.

Bright Smile Dickson, 1980. 'Eurorose' × seedling
Very healthy, shining green leaves and good, bushy, upright growth to 60cm (2ft). The medium-sized flowers come in small trusses and are a bright, fresh yellow of singular purity. They eventually open wide, giving a brilliant mass display.

Cameo De Ruiter, 1932. Sport from 'Orléans Rose' and hence a true Polyantha
Clear salmon-pink, semi-double, cupped flowers in good-sized clusters on a bushy plant with bright green foliage. Will grow anywhere, even in some shade, but a watch must be kept for mildew.

Cha Cha Cocker, 1983. ('Wee Man' × 'Manx Queen') × 'Darling Flame'
Growing to 45cm (18in), this rose has slightly fragrant, semi-double flowers, in colour red with a yellow eye. Fairly dense growth and good, medium green foliage.

Cider Cup Dickson, 1988. 'Memento' seedling
Hybrid Tea-shaped 5cm (2in) blooms of deep apricot, carried all summer on a bushy plant. Small, semi-glossy leaves and a slight fragrance. Its exceptional continuity of bloom is clearly inherited from its outstanding parent, as those who have grown the latter will know.

Clarissa Harkness, 1983. 'Southampton' × 'Darling Flame'
Only ten patio roses described so far and already the miniature rose 'Darling Flame' has appeared in the parentage of three of them, which says something for its qualities. 'Clarissa' is a little on the tall side and rather upright in growth for a patio rose, being only moderately bushy, making it ideal for lining a path where the space is very limited. It carries large trusses of immaculately shaped blooms in apricot shades and has healthy, shiny foliage. It will blend well in a mixed border.

Conservation Cocker, 1988. [('Sabine' × 'Circus') × 'Maxi'] × 'Darling Flame'
Blooms in blends of salmon-red and apricot, not fully double but opening

wide in the most appealing way. Large, well-spaced trusses on compact plants with fine dark, glossy leaves. A pleasing fragrance of fresh hay and a spreading habit. One of the best of recent roses.

Coral Reef Cocker, 1986. Parentage not given
A bushy, 45cm (18in) plant bearing prettily formed, orange-coral, semi-double flowers and healthy, glossy leaves.

Dainty Dinah Cocker 1981. 'Anne Cocker' × 'Wee Man'
Salmon-pink blooms, shapely at first and then opening wide in fine, showy clusters. Bushy and spreading with mid-green, semi-glossy leaves that may need protection from black spot. Maximum height is about 45cm (18in).

Dopey De Ruiter, 1954. Parentage not given
Another of the Seven Dwarfs roses which, as a group, went under the name Compacta. This one is crimson-scarlet with semi-double flowers in large trusses on a bushy plant.

Dr McAlpine Pearce, 1982. Parentage not given
Raised by an amateur but available from the rose trade, this one has fragrant, deep rose-pink blooms on a strong-growing plant that will reach 38cm (15in) or so and has dark, shiny foliage.

Drummer Boy Harkness, 1987. Seedling × 'Red Sprite'
Neat and bushy, the plants of this form cushions of the brightest crimson, which is quite unfading whatever the weather conditions. The winner of a Certificate of Merit in the Dublin Rose Trials and certainly a rose with a future.

Eblouissant Turbat, 1918. Unknown rose × 'Cramoisi Supérieur'
An interesting Polyantha with very double, globular flowers in a deep, striking red and with a slight fragrance. The leaves are glossy and a bronze-green, covering the bushy, low-growing plant well. Not stocked by everybody, but worth trying for.

Edith Cavell (Miss Edith Cavell) De Ruiter, 1917. Sport of 'Orléans Rose'
A Polyantha with full, globular, scarlet blooms, overlaid with velvety crimson and carried in good-sized clusters and in great profusion. Leathery, glossy leaves that may need watching for mildew.

The Fairy Bentall, 1932. 'Paul Crampel' × 'Lady Gay'
This is not the parentage that you will find in many early books because

this rose was long considered to be a sport of the rambler 'Lady Godiva'. A member of the Bentall family has put us right, for which we are indebted as this is an important rose, being one of the few old-style Polyanthas that is still really popular and widely grown. Its good qualities include huge trusses of small, double pink blooms which are carried right through the summer, backed by bright green, glossy foliage on a bushy plant of spreading habit. Makes a fine low hedge, but black spot cannot be ruled out.

Frankenland Tantau, 1978. Parentage not given
For those who know 'Topsi', this is not dissimilar, though it is a good deal more healthy and thus probably the better bet if you can get hold of it. The flowers are shapely in the bud but open wide. They are coral-orange. The plant has a good bushy habit and will grow to 30cm (12in) or so. It has unusually pale green leaves.

Frau Astrid Späth, Späth 1930. Polyantha sport of 'Lafayette'
Clear carmine-rose, double and rather globular flowers in good clusters on a dwarf, bushy plant with dark, glossy leaves. This rose has, in its turn, sported a striped version.

Fresh Pink Moore, 1964. (*R. wichuraiana* × 'Floradora') × 'Little Buckaroo'
Clear pink, double flowers in sizeable clusters. They develop from rounded buds and open cupped. Profuse in bloom and with a slight fragrance. Vigorous and bushy with leathery, glossy leaves. One from that great raiser of miniatures that turned out to be really more of a patio rose.

Garnette Tantau, 1951. ('Rosenelfe' × 'Eva') × 'Heros'
This is a rose which I have hesitated about including as it is rather on the tall side and popularly supposed to be too mildew-prone for garden use. For long it was a great favourite with the cut-flower trade because of the long-lasting qualities of its very double, rosette-type blooms, and I have found that, at least on my light soil, 'Garnette' is perfectly satisfactory in the open. It makes an excellent container plant for a patio, and the very double, deep carmine-red flowers have exceptionally thick petals, which probably accounts for their long-lasting qualities. They are carried in large and small trusses on a well-branched plant that will reach 75cm (2½ft). Dark, leathery, rather holly-like leaves complete the picture. This is the original rose of a group listed below, all of them broadly similar, though some of them without the true 'Garnette' parentage.

Garnette Apricot
Yellow with pink flushes.

Garnette Carol
A true sport of 'Garnette' with light pink flowers.

Garnette Pink Chiffon
Larger flowers than the type and is a pleasing blush-pink.

Garnette Rose
Deep carmine-pink.

Garnette Yellow
Pale Yellow.

Gentle Touch Dickson, 1986. 'Liverpool Echo' × ('Woman's Own' × 'Memento')
The Rose Growers' Association Rose of the Year for 1986, which means that it was picked as the best rose for that season by British rose nurserymen, a considerable accolade when one considers how many new varieties are introduced in the course of twelve months. Far too many, of course, but this was a good one and the first patio rose to gain such an award. It is a bushy, short grower with small, only moderately full, pale pink blooms in medium-sized but plentiful clusters. Almost the whole of the plant will be covered with the pleasantly fragrant flowers at any one time.

Ginger Nut Cocker, 1988. ('Sabine' × 'Circus') × 'Darling Flame'
A startling new colour for a patio rose and the only one of its kind. The neat double flowers, which open flat, are a bronze-orange with a reddish reverse to the petals. Good, evenly spaced clusters come with great freedom and good continuity on a compact plant with rather small, glossy leaves.

Gloire du Midi De Ruiter, 1932. 'Gloria Mundi' sport and hence a Polyantha
Leathery foliage covers this vigorous but compact plant which carries its small, double, globular, slightly fragrant, brilliant orange-scarlet flowers on good-sized trusses. Mildew, unfortunately, cannot be ruled out.

Gloria Mundi De Ruiter, 1929. Sport of 'Superb', itself a De Ruiter Polyantha of 1927, the 'parentage' of which reinforces what I said at the beginning of this chapter about the possible disadvantages of planting the old Polyanthas due to this tendency to sport. You never know when it may happen and you may well get a sport yourself, which can be either annoying or exciting, according to how you look at it. At any rate, 'Gloria Mundi' was one of the best and best-known of the De Ruiter

Polyanthas of the late 1920s and 1930s. Vigorous and bushy to 60cm (2ft), with striking, orange-scarlet flowers, not too unlike in colour the much later 'Super Star', and light green, glossy foliage that must be watched for mildew. There are two different and distinct climbing sports of this rose.

Golden Salmon De Ruiter, 1926. Sport of 'Superb'
Same parentage as 'Gloria Mundi' but more orange and less red in the flowers, which come in truly enormous trusses. It sported in its turn to produce 'Golden Salmon Supérieur'.

Grumpy De Ruiter, 1956. Parentage not given
Very bushy with good trusses of small, double, pink flowers. Another of the Compacta roses.

Happy De Ruiter, 1954. 'Robin Hood' × 'Katharina Zeimet' seedling
Another Compacta with very small, semi-double, currant-red flowers in large trusses. Dark, glossy leaves.

Honeybunch Cocker, 1989. Seedling × 'Bright Smile'
Growing to 45cm (18in) and with a pleasant scent, this bush carries well-formed flowers of honey-yellow with a touch here and there of salmon-pink. Excellent for freedom of flowering and makes good cut flowers.

International Herald Tribune Harkness, 1985. Unnamed seedling × [('Orange Sensation' × 'Allgold') × *R. californica*)]
A bright, intense purple characterises the flowers of this rose and they are carried in good-sized clusters on a spreading bush of rather open growth. They are scented and fairly full. Will probably reach 45–60cm (1½–2ft). Makes a decorative hedge and blends particularly well with pink roses.

Jane Asher Pearce, 1987. Parentage not given
Only 25–38cm (10–14in) high, this one has double flowers in brilliant scarlet carried over a very long season and almost without pause. A fine health record goes with this smallest of the patio roses.

Jean Mermoz Chenault, 1937. *R. wichuraiana* × a Hybrid Tea
A very low-growing Polyantha with double, imbricated, slightly fragrant, light pink flowers in corymb-like clusters. Foliage glossy and dark green. A very vigorous grower and something rather different.

Katharina Zeimet Lambert, 1901. Parentage not known
A Polyantha with clusters of pure white flowers on a stocky, twiggy plant with bright green, glossy leaves. The blooms have a sweet fragrance.

Kim Harkness, 1973. ('Orange Sensation' × 'Allgold') × 'Elizabeth of Glamis'
The flowers, which open flat, are very large for a plant that will only reach 45cm (18in) and are yellow suffused with pink. It repeats well and makes an excellent cut flower. A strong, bushy grower.

Leonie Lamesch Lambert Lambert, 1899. Parentage not known
Included with some trepidation and only because of its novelty as the soft foliage will certainly need spraying against mildew. Semi-double, light coppery-red flowers with yellow centres and darker flecking on the petal edges. Bushy and on the tall side, but do try it in an odd corner.

Little Jewel Cocker, 1980. 'Wee Man' × 'Belinda'
Bushy and vigorous, it bears plentiful, bright rose-pink flowers of a pleasing rosette shape. At 45cm (18in) will make a very good pot plant.

Little Prince Cocker, 1983. 'Darling Flame' × ('National Trust' × 'Wee Man')
Always in flower and a startling bright orange-red. A compact, upright bush with healthy leaves.

Little White Pet (White Pet) Henderson, 1879
Not one of the very early Polyanthas as might have been expected from its appearance, but a dwarf sport of the Sempervirens rambler 'Félicité Perpétue'. It seldom tops 60cm (2ft) and is almost continuously in bloom. Its creamy-white, rosette-shaped flowers are carried in large clusters and it has remained unsurpassed by any other white rose in its class.

Little Woman Dickson, 1987. Parentage not given
The buds have an appealing urn shape like those of a miniature Hybrid Tea, and are carried in well-spaced trusses. The colour is basically a pretty shade of pink but varies somewhat according to the time of year, though it is always attractive. There is some fragrance and it is an upright, bushy grower to about 45cm (18in).

Marie Pavie Alegatiere, 1888. Parentage not known
An early Polyantha and long-time favourite for its fine clusters of blush-white, double flowers carried on a bushy, 45cm (18in) plant with exceptionally large, fresh green leaves.

Marlena Kordes, 1964. 'Gertrude Westphal' × 'Lilli Marlene'
Despite the possibility of black spot, this has long been and remains one of the best of the patio roses, coming on the scene long before the term patio rose was even thought of. It has medium-sized clusters of

moderately full, bright crimson but unfortunately scentless flowers, which are carried with great freedom and outstanding continuity. Bushy to 60cm (2ft) and clothed with glossy, deep green leaves. There are few nurseries that do not stock it.

Mignonette Guillot Fils, 1880. Possibly a second generation cross between *R. chinensis* and *R. multiflora*
This is very free-blooming and carries large clusters of very small, soft pink flowers which will soon fade to white. Whether or not you can find space in a small garden for such curiosities is a matter of personal choice, but this was probably the first Polyantha of all and hence the first to approach the concept of a patio rose. Only stocked by specialist growers.

Minilights Dickson, 1988. Parentage not given
Something rather different from those so far described, as it will only reach about 25cm (10in) but will spread out to about twice that distance, making a fine cushion of colour with its attractive sprays of single, yellow flowers and bright, shiny leaves. Seldom out of bloom throughout the summer.

Nathalie Nypels (Mevrouw Nathalie Nypels) Leenders, 1919. 'Orléans Rose' × ('Comtesse du Cayla' × *R. foetida bicolor*)
An interesting Polyantha/China rose/species cross which has produced one of the most free-flowering roses ever and one which has maintained its popularity for seventy years. The very fragrant, medium-sized, semi-double flowers in soft rose-pink are carried on a low-growing but spreading bush and the dark green leaves have a good health record. Thoroughly recommended.

Nypels Perfection Leenders, 1930. Parentage not known
A much later Polyantha from the raiser of the one above and one which, despite its name, does not eclipse 'Nathalie Nypels'. It is, however, still a good rose with large, semi-double, hydrangea-pink flowers, flushed a deeper pink. Bushy and reaching 60cm (2ft).

Paul Crampel Kersbergen, 1930. Parentage not known
A vintage Polyantha from the heyday of the family and rather resembling 'Gloria Mundi' with its orange-scarlet flowers, which are probably rather brighter, certainly larger, but not so double. Several climbing sports have been recorded.

Peek A Boo Dickson, 1981. 'Memento' × 'Nozomi'
One of the earliest of the new generation of patio roses, low and spreading, making an attractive mound with its large clusters of moder-

ately full, soft apricot-pink flowers. Still one of the best of its class with an RNRS award to prove it. A good health record. Not much scent.

Penelope Keith (Freegold) McGredy, 1984. Parentage not given
Growing to 60cm (2ft), this rose carries its small, bright yellow flowers in medium-sized clusters with considerable freedom and good continuity. An upright stance and not as spreading as some, it makes a compact plant with healthy, mid-green leaves.

Petit Four Ilsink, 1982. 'Marlena' seedling × seedling
If it was not for all the others which are just as good, this could be called the perfect bedding rose for the small garden with its neat, 38cm (15in) growth and bushy, spreading habit. The small, semi-double flowers in full flush almost obscure the bright, shiny foliage and are a luminous, clear pink with paler centres.

Pink Posy Cocker, 1983. 'Trier' × 'New Penny'
'Trier' was the rose that started off the Hybrid Musks and it is interesting to see it used again here, crossed with a miniature to produce a 38–45cm (15–18in) bush with very small, double flowers in a light, rosy-pink. Free-flowering and with a carnation-like scent, this is something rather out of the ordinary. Dark green, matt leaves.

Pink Sunblaze (Pink Meillandina) Meilland, 1983. Sport of 'Orange Sunblaze'
Double, cupped, bright pink flowers borne in profusion in small clusters. A dense, bushy grower with light green, matt foliage on which mildew is a possibility.

Ray of Sunshine Cocker, 1988. 'Korresia' × seedling
With a height of about 38cm (15in), this has slightly fragrant, clear, bright, unfading yellow flowers on a nice bushy plant, the small shiny leaves of which enhance the semi-double blooms. It was named to celebrate the 7th Anniversary of the Sunshine Fund for Blind Babies and Young People.

Red Rascal Warriner, 1988. Parentage not known
An American contribution to the patio rose family and a very good one. It makes a compact bush with dark green leaves which set off the bright scarlet-crimson flowers which have a satiny sheen to the petals. A compact bush with dark green leaves.

Regensberg (Young Mistress, Buffalo Bill) McGredy, 1979. 'Geoff Boycott' × 'Old Master'

The flowers of this one are very unusual, pale pink, edged white and with a white eye, together with a white petal reverse, one colour 'feathering' into the other in a manner typical of the McGredy 'Hand Painted' roses, of which this is a very neat, low-growing example. A good front-of-the-border rose, though black spot cannot be ruled out.

Robin Redbreast Ilsink, 1984. Seedling × 'Eye Paint'
The flowers are not unlike those of the second parent, single, dark red and with creamy-yellow centres and a silvery reverse. Fine, glossy foliage on thorny stems which make up a bushy, spreading plant about 45cm (18in) in height.

Rosabell Cocker, 1988. Seedling × 'Darling Flame'
Where would patio roses be without the firm of James Cocker of Aberdeen, and for that matter without Pat Dickson of Northern Ireland? Here is yet another Cocker variety, once again using 'Darling Flame' as a parent, this time resulting in a bushy, 38cm (15in) plant of spreading growth and with dark, glossy leaves and flowers with over 60 petals each, some 8cm (3in) across, rose-pink and quartered like the best of the old garden roses. A wild rose perfume adds to its attractions.

Scottish Special Cocker, 1987. 'Wee Man' × 'Darling Flame'
A pretty rose with semi-double flowers in apple blossom-pink and peach, carried on a low, rounded bush with healthy, mid-green foliage. Constantly in flower.

Sleepy De Ruiter, 1955. ('Orange Triumph' × 'Golden Rapture') × Polyantha seedling
Another of the Compacta roses, this time with double, reddish-pink flowers.

Sneezy (Bertram) de Ruiter, 1955. Parentage not given
The last of the seven Compacta roses with small, single, rose-pink blooms.

Star Child Dickson, 1988. 'Eye Paint' × seedling
Flowers of twelve petals and 5cm (2in) across, orange-scarlet and ivory at the petal bases and on the reverse. Very striking indeed; a real eyecatcher. It will reach about 45cm (18in) in height and make a bushy plant with plentiful, healthy, glossy leaves. A winner of many Gold and other medals.

Stargazer Harkness, 1977. 'Marlena' × 'Kim'
Bushy and short with single blooms in good-sized clusters, orange-scarlet with a yellow centre, the scarlet fading to carmine after a while. Only slight fragrance, but good, shiny leaves.

String of Pearls Rearsby Roses, 1985. Parentage not given
On this one the leaves are deep purple on opening and gradually turn to a pleasing dark green, forming a fine background for the flowers. These change colour, too, opening coppery-pink, becoming pearly-pink and finally fading to white. They open wide to show off their orange-yellow stamens. Neat and compact at 45cm (18in).

Sweet Dream Fryer, 1988. Parentage not given
Voted the RGA Rose of the Year for 1988, this is a small, bushy grower with full-petalled, peachy-apricot flowers in short-stemmed clusters. The foliage is plentiful, mid-green and semi-glossy,

Sweet Magic Dickson, 1987. Parentage not given
This and the previous rose reflect the growing prestige of patio roses, for this was the RGA Rose of the Year for 1987. The tiny blooms come from Hybrid Tea-style buds, opening to show a full boss of stamens which match the flower colour exactly—orange with golden tints. The leaves are mid-green and glossy and the habit bushy and spreading.

Sweet Symphonie Meilland, 1989. 'Meigurami' × 'Magic Carrousel'
Hot off the press one might say comes this one, the RNRS President's International Trophy winner for the best new rose of the year in 1989. This means that it has excelled in the St Albans trials and there should be no reason why it should not do equally well in general garden use—but it has not had time to do so yet. That said, buy it for its lovely clusters of moderately full, scented, pink flowers which come in good clusters on a low bush of dense habit and a good health record.

Tip Top Tantau, 1963. Parentage unknown
Back in the 1960s, 'Tip Top' could really be said to have set the pattern for the modern patio rose, for the style of its flowers is much more in the modern idiom than that of the older Polyanthas. They are carried in sizeable trusses, semi-double, the colour being a rosy-salmon-pink. A trend-setter, but not, unfortunately, a very healthy one.

Topsi Tantau, 1972. 'Fragrant Cloud' × 'Fire Signal'
Of the most startling and eyecatching orange-scarlets, 'Topsi''s semi-double blooms are carried in fair-sized trusses on very short stems. 'Fragrant Cloud' passed on none of its scent to this offspring. A rose that

has remained popular because of its colour, though its very brightness means that care is needed in placing it in the garden. It is, too, very prone to both black spot and die-back.

Trumpeter McGredy, 1978. 'Satchmo' × seedling
A rose with cheerful, orange-red flowers in great profusion, so much so at times that the comparatively short stems are bowed down almost to the ground by the weight of the trusses after rain. However, it still puts on a brave show and the plant in general is compact enough and bushes out well to about 60cm (2ft).

Warrior Le Grice, 1978. 'City of Belfast' × 'Ronde Endiablée'
Introduced in the same year as 'Trumpeter' and remarkably similar to it, with the same short growth and bright red, double flowers. Both roses can be thoroughly recommended and it is difficult to put one before the other, though 'Warrior''s Trial Ground Certificate at the RNRS Trials did not quite match the Certificate of Merit awarded to 'Trumpeter'.

Wee Jock Cocker, 1980. 'National Trust' × 'Wee Man'
Fully double, bright crimson-scarlet flowers in sizeable clusters on a plant with mid-green, glossy foliage and a compact, bushy habit. Very free-flowering but only a slight fragrance.

Wishing Dickson, 1985. 'Silver Jubilee' × 'Bright Smile'
Two first-rate roses have produced another, the flowers of which might almost be those of 'Silver Jubilee' in miniature, having the same classic shape and deep, salmon-pink colouring. Perhaps they could come a little more freely, but the repeat is quite good and the plant bushy and upright with fine, glossy leaves.

Yvonne Rabier Turbat, 1910. *R. wichuraiana* × a Polyantha
A rose so good in most ways that it has never lost its popularity with the more discerning rose grower. A typical Polyantha in most ways, it is a short, bushy grower with clusters of moderately full, white blooms and shiny, green leaves. Unlike most Polyanthas, however, it is sweetly scented. A strong recommendation.

CHAPTER 3

SMALL SHRUB ROSES

This chapter will describe and discuss a wide-ranging group of roses, using them to show just how versatile in the garden the rose family can be. However, first of all it would be as well to establish what is meant by the term shrub rose since all roses are, by dictionary definition, shrubs. It is a term, recognised as a completely artificial one with no botanical validity, which has been found useful to describe all those roses (excluding climbers and miniatures) which, by reason of their size or their habit of growth, are unsuitable for bedding. In other words some are too big or too lax, too wide-spreading or in other ways lack the uniformity necessary to make good bedding plants in the way that Floribundas and Hybrid Tea roses do.

The enormously wide range of roses included under the name shrub rose means that it is impossible to produce a potted history which embraces them all. They include roses introduced so long ago that nobody knows the date when they first arrived on the garden scene or where they came from, a few of which have been included in our selection for reasons given later in the chapter, but the majority covered here are much more modern and many have only just been introduced. Among the latter have been included the so-called ground-cover roses, or at least the less rampant ones, for quite frankly they are simply low-growing, spreading shrubs with hardly more power to blanket the ground and smother weeds than a Floribunda or Hybrid Tea of spreading habit. It is a pity that claims have been put forward for some of them that they cannot fulfil, for they are perfectly good roses in their own right. They are small shrub roses and, if left to themselves, would not pretend to be anything else.

As it is not possible to give a general historical background, the next best thing would seem to be to run through the descriptive list of roses that follows this introduction, picking out points of historical or other special interest as and where they occur and, even more important, giving some idea of the uses to which some of them can be put in the garden. Take, for instance, the second on the list, 'Angelina', with which could be bracketed the third, 'Anna Zinkeisen', 'Ferdy', 'Mary Hayley Bell', 'Red Blanket', 'Rosy Cushion', 'Fru Dagmar Hastrup' and 'Smarty'. All of them are reasonably compact shrubs, not too tall—up to 1.2m (4ft) or so, which will make admirable garden features if grown on their own, but can be even better if planted in groups of three, perhaps in a round bed cut in a lawn, or else filling in the angle where two paths meet. If placed near a path, however, they should be at least 1m (3ft) away from it to allow for their sideways spread. Wet leaves, to say nothing of wet blooms brushing against the legs on a rainy morning, are something to be avoided, as has already been pointed out.

These seven roses are, in addition, quite informal enough in their habit of growth to be used as foreground planting for other shrubs or in a mixed border of herbaceous perennials. For at least four of them claims have been made as to their ground-covering capacity which do not bear much resemblance to reality, but as against this, with 'Fru Dagmar Hastrup' there is a bonus. It has large and decorative hips which follow the flowers and, as it is remontant, both will appear on the plant at the same time.

Equally good for mixing with other plants (see Chapter 9) are some of the really old roses such as the Gallica 'Belle de Crécy', The Burgundian Rose which, with 'Petite de Hollande' is a member of the Centifolia group but much smaller than most, 'Officinalis', 'Rosa Mundi' and the Portland rose, 'Rose de Rescht'. These are interesting to grow, not only for their beautiful flowers but for their historical associations, but 'Rose de Rescht' is the only one that will flower again after midsummer. Once flowering is not, of course, confined to roses as many other plants do not flower more than once in a season, but with roses there is always the alternative, in that one can grow modern varieties. There is also a compromise which, for the lover of old rose styles, is a possible solution.

Comparatively recently a whole new range of varieties known as English roses have been introduced by their creator, David Austin. These reproduce most of the features of the old roses, but have a much wider range of colours and are remontant into the bargain. We will discuss them in rather more detail in a moment, but first a little should be said about growing the older ones which, there is no doubt about it, have a fascination all their own which none of the moderns can match.

'Officinalis' is probably the oldest cultivated rose we know, going back at least to the sixteenth century. At one time it was extensively grown for medicinal purposes, extracts from its petals, hips and roots being used to cure pretty well every ailment under the sun. Thus it became known as The Apothecary's Rose, and it is also believed to be the original Red Rose of Lancaster from the Wars of the Roses. No modern rose could flaunt a pedigree like that.

'Officinalis' is compact enough to make an attractive low hedge, and the same can be said for its sport, 'Rosa Mundi', which has the gayest of flowers, quite loosely formed but with the petals striped in dark pink on the palest of blush-pink backgrounds. When used for hedges the pair of them, neither of which will go much over 1.2m (4ft), can be clipped over in the winter rather than pruned in the conventional manner. However, the natural outline of the bushes should be followed and no attempt made to shape them formally like a box or privet hedge. 'Rose de Rescht' grows in much the same way as the two Gallicas, though it is probably rather smaller and is continuous in its flowering. Its deep red blooms are absolutely crammed with petals and they come with considerable freedom.

So, too, do the flowers of the three small Centifolias, The Burgundian Rose, 'Petite de Hollande' and 'De Meaux', but their habit of growth is very different. Their small, globular blooms hang like miniature lanterns from gently arching shoots on open-growing shrubs that look particularly well in a mixed border.

These few are just a very small selection of moderately sized old garden roses suitable for a small garden, and for those not used to growing them perhaps a few general points about them might be of value. Their flowers are different from those of most modern roses. There is none of the high, conical centre that wins prizes for the best Hybrid Teas on the show benches and is to be found as well in a number of Floribundas. The blooms are mostly globular or cupped in shape, at least on opening. They have many petals, which usually reflex after a while so that the blooms open flat, the petals infolded to give a quartered effect. Sometimes the stamens can be seen, but often the flowers are too double for this. The colours range from white, through a wide range of pinks, to maroon, crimson and purple. There are no yellows, though these may be found among some of the species roses which consort so well with the old garden ones.

Few of the old garden roses have glossy leaves. Some, typified by the Alba rose 'Félicité Parmentier' in our selection, have foliage of the most attractive soft, grey-green, which makes a wonderful foil for the soft pink flowers and looks good after the flowers have gone. This cannot be said, however, about the leaves of all the old roses. In general they do not age particularly well and for this reason, if your space is limited by a small garden and unless you are a real and dedicated enthusiast, this might be an added reason to take heed of the warning sounded in Chapter 1 and possibly forget them.

Try instead the English roses referred to earlier and our selection has been made to include only those of modest size. They mostly make reasonably upright shrubs with fairly slender canes which tend to be bowed down by the weight of the large, richly sumptuous blooms. An exception to this is Austin's 'Yellow Button', which makes a small, sturdy bush more in the style of the Polyantha roses. It will make a cushion of the brightest yellow and if a number are run together they will make a fine edging. One alone will spread out enough to fill a round bed 1m (3ft) across, making a striking specimen planting. Or try it in a round tub.

Much the same could be said about many of the other roses in our selection, varieties like 'Ballerina', 'Bonica', 'Corylus' (which has orange hips to follow the flowers), The Dunwich Rose (which, being a near species, only flowers once a year). 'Grüss an Aachen', 'Hampshire', 'Marjorie Fair' (a darker-coloured 'Ballerina'), 'Suffolk' and 'Tamora' (another David Austin rose and the raiser's choice as the best of his roses for a small garden). Where you might have considered putting four or five Floribundas in a group, one of these roses can be used instead, with probably more continuous bloom into the bargain. With small shrubs one begins to think in drifts and banks of colour rather than in formal beds, in curved edges to borders rather than straight lines.

Even more economical will be our next batch of roses, typified by 'Candy Rose', 'Essex', 'Eyeopener', 'La Sevillana', 'Pearl Drift', 'Pink Drift', 'Raubritter' and 'Running Maid', for these will not go much above 60cm–1m (2–3ft) in height but will spread out a good deal further than that. So too will 'Red Bells', 'Pink Bells' and 'White Bells', which have a much denser covering of leaves than most so that they are real weed smotherers, but which, despite being modern hybrids, flower only at midsummer. That drawback has been overcome with the more recent County series, which can give equally good ground cover when grown at their best. They are ideal if you have spaces which need filling quickly or if your garden has a difficult area such as a bank where only rank grass can be persuaded to follow spring bulbs. The roses, planted in properly prepared ground at the top, will tumble down the bank and if they have been put in close enough together so that the branches of one can intertwine with those of another, may even cause the rank grass to wilt. Soon the earth beneath will have vanished completely.

From the detailed descriptions that follow an idea will be gained of the size that will be achieved by each variety, enabling planting distances to be calculated. At the same time it must not be forgotten that a great many factors can affect the ultimate size of a rose bush—climate, soil, cultivation and the quality of the original plant can all influence it, so that any measurements which are given should be taken as an informed guess, not a definite statement of fact.

Other roses that spread out well but are much more open and airy in habit include the fairy series raised by Jack Harkness. 'Fairy Changeling', 'Fairy Damsel' and 'Fairyland', together with 'Fairy Prince' which is the most wide-spreading of all and which needs to be planted about 1.2m (4ft) apart, are examples from this group. One can bracket with them such roses as 'Cécile Brunner' (in its bush form) and 'Yesterday', also of

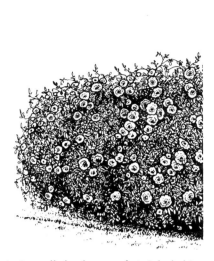

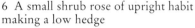

6 A small shrub rose of upright habit making a low hedge

7 A typical small shrub rose tumbling over a wall

Harkness raising. The latter is probably the smallest of this small group and the flowers are of a rosy-magenta rather than the pink variations of the other five.

It is difficult nowadays to keep pace with the new roses in this category as they appear in increasing numbers each year. Quite obviously rose growers have taken them to their hearts, for their virtues are many and they make a refreshing change from what has gone before: Incredible freedom of flowering and continuity make them quite outstanding, with economy of use due to the amount of ground each bush will cover, and the weed-smothering properties of a few of them, adding to a formidable list of good points. With a number little if any pruning need be done and in most cases only dead or diseased wood may be removed with, perhaps, some shortening of the side shoots. That alone should be enough to ensure them a rapturous welcome.

A number of these small shrub roses are sold in standard form, and for my money they are infinitely preferable to the standards formed from Hybrid Teas or Floribundas which so often look unbalanced and clumsy. The thinner, laxer and more twiggy growth of so many of the smaller shrub roses makes for much more attractive standard heads, and with some of them the shoots are long and flexible enough to emulate weeping standards, than which, at their best, there is nothing lovelier.

Varieties of shrub roses

Alba Meidiland Meilland, 1987. Parentage unknown
Vigorous and spreading, this is one of several roses that are ideal for covering a difficult slope. No more than 60cm (2 ft) high, it will form a dense carpet up to 1.2m (4ft) across, covered in large clusters of pure white, double flowers that last well if cut for the house. Semi-glossy, dark green leaves.

Angelina Cocker, 1975. ('Super Star' × 'Carina') × ('Cläre Grammer-storf' × 'Frühlingsmorgen')
A most attractive small shrub reaching 1–1.2m (3–4ft) in height and 1m (3ft) across. The blooms, in small clusters, are quite large, semi-double opening wide, and pale pink with a white eye. They rather resemble those of 'Complicata' but on a smaller scale, but they are, unlike those of the larger rose, fully remontant. They come at all levels on a compact, bushy shrub which deserves to be much better known than it is.

Anna Zinkeisen Harkness, 1983. Seedling × 'Frank Naylor'
This makes a bushy, rather spreading shrub about 1–1.2m (3–4ft) high carrying medium-sized flowers with a multitude of petals in the old-rose style. Sometimes they come one to a stem, but more often they are in clusters of variable size. Opening from yellow buds to the creamy-ivory of the fully expanded flower, they have a sweet musk fragrance and there is excellent continuity throughout the summer and autumn. Light green, semi-glossy foliage.

Ballerina Bentall, 1937. Parentage unknown
This is often classed as a Hybrid Musk but only, it would seem, because it came from the Pemberton/Bentall stable. It is low-growing and spreading, with huge sprays of very small, single flowers that resemble nothing so much as apple blossom in their mixture of pink and white colourings. At its most vigorous it can reach 1.2m (4ft), but can be kept lower. At its best it can be magnificent, with shiny green foliage to back up the display of flowers. However, when black spot attacks this rose it seems to do so with unwonted speed and a bush can be rapidly defoliated.

Belle de Crécy Date of introduction unknown
This is the first of the old garden roses included in this section and makes the point very well that by no means all of the early shrub roses are too big for a small garden. It will seldom top 1.2m (4ft), but its small size is not, of course, the only reason for recommending it. Nearly thornless, its lax, arching branches bear flowers (at midsummer only) which are some of the most beautiful of all. They open a rich, purplish-pink which

changes quite soon to a mixture of purple-lilac, slate-grey and wild-rose-pink. They are backed by rather dull green leaves, which are quite typical of the rose family to which this belongs, the Gallicas. It is a rose that may need some support.

Bonica (Demon) Meilland, 1982. (*R. sempervirens* × 'Mlle Marthe Carron') × 'Picasso'
Why this rose's alternative name should be 'Demon' it is impossible to imagine, for it makes one of the prettiest and gentlest of sights in the garden. It forms a spreading, arching shrub up to 1m (3ft) tall with a dense cover of small, shiny, very healthy leaves and medium-sized clusters of double, light pink flowers, the colour of which intensifies as they age. They are carried over a long period and the rose is fully remontant. Plant a few together and they will cover the ground so thoroughly that no weed beneath them would stand a chance.

The Burgundian Rose (Pompon de Bourgogne, *R. centifolia* 'Parvifolia'). Age and origin unknown
A member of the Centifolia family and so once-flowering only, but when it does the 60 × 60cm (2 × 2ft) bush is covered in 3cm (1in) rosette blooms of rosy-purple, some flecked with pink. Growth is untypically erect, with stiff stems and with leaves more pointed than is usual with a Centifolia. A real beauty.

Candy Rose Meilland, 1980. (*R. sempervirens* × 'Mlle Martha Carron') × [('Lilli Marlene' × 'Evelyn Fison') × ('Orange Sweetheart' × 'Frühlingsmorgen')]
A complicated parentage has produced a lax but bushy shrub that will not top 1.2m (4ft) but will spread out to about 1.8m (6ft) across, though it is not really dense enough for complete ground cover. It carries its flowers, semi-double and deep pink, paling in the centre and with a much deeper pink reverse, in small clusters but with great profusion. The leaves are small, light green and glossy. This is one you must make sure you have space for. It gives very good value, being fully remontant, but it does take up a lot of space.

Cardinal Hume Harkness, 1984. [[Seedling × ('Orange Sensation' × 'Allgold')] × *R. californica*] × 'Frank Naylor'
Reaching 1m (3ft) or so and spreading out rather more, this rose carries dark Tyrian purple, double, cupped flowers in large clusters. They are held close to the plant on short stems, seeming to nestle into the leaves. A good scent adds to the attraction and, though modern, this variety fits in well with the old roses, except that it is remontant. The leaves are dark green and pointed. Some mildew possible.

Cécile Brunner (Mignon, the Sweetheart Rose) Pernet-Ducher, 1881. A Polyantha × 'Mme de Tartas'
The parentage makes this a Tea-Polyantha though it is sometimes grouped with the China roses, largely, it would seem, because it rather resembles a China rose in its airy habit of growth.

The tiny, thimble-sized blooms are of classic shape in the bud but open rather loosely. They are soft flesh-pink, deeper in the centre, and are carried freely in small sprays throughout the summer and autumn. A pretty rose but never a showy one, and the flowers have little scent. The bush will reach 60cm (2ft) in height and spreads out well so that it will make a good bedding rose where something quiet and restrained is wanted. The dark green leaves are semi-glossy and very healthy. Strangely for so small a rose, its climbing sport is incredibly vigorous and will scale a 6m (20ft) tree with ease. It is much too strong-growing to be included in the climber selection of this book, which is a pity because it is a real beauty if you can accommodate it.

Corylus Le Rougetel, 1988. *R. rugosa* × *R. nitida*
An interesting hybrid between two good species, each of which has contributed towards 'Corylus''s fine qualities. It is a very dense, bushy grower reaching about 1 × 1m (3 × 3ft), with light green, feathery foliage. Bright, orange-red hips follow the flowers, which are carried continuously throughout the summer and are silvery-pink with a fine boss of stamens. The yellow, autumn tints of the foliage (a Rugosa inheritance) make a striking show when combined with the hips. When on its own roots this rose will spread rapidly by underground suckers, a point not to be overlooked when considering it for a small garden.

De Meaux Raiser not known; date of introduction probably 1814
A Centifolia and, like The Burgundian Rose, by no means a conventional one. It forms a bush much more erect than is usual with this family and which, though still arching, will only reach about 107cm (3½ft) in height. It has small, light green foliage and the light pink, 3cm (1in) flowers pass through the pompom stage before finally opening flat. Sweetly scented, they appear early in June and there is no repeat. However, blooming will be enhanced by reasonably hard pruning and the thinning out of twiggy shoots.

The Dunwich Rose (*R. dunwichensis*) Form of *R. pimpinellifolia* found growing on sand dunes at the village of Dunwich in Suffolk in 1956
It will make a mounding bush some 60cm (2ft) tall by 1.2m (4ft) wide, covered with light green, fern-like foliage and soft yellow, single flowers with a great boss of yellow stamens but only a slight fragrance. They are produced singly all along the arching, thorny shoots and appear at

midsummer only. The attractive foliage, however, is a very adequate substitute after the flowers have gone. Like all the Burnet or Scotch roses, which are popular names for the Pimpinellifolias, it will spread by suckers with the speed of light if it is on its own roots.

English Garden Austin, 1986. ('Lilian Austin' × unnamed seedling) × ('Iceberg' × 'Wife of Bath')
At 1m × 60cm (3 × 2ft), this could be used as a bedding rose, but it loses something if grown in the mass. Rather it should be displayed in such a way that the full beauty of its individual blooms can be fully appreciated. A group of only three or four would be ideal for this, a feature on its own.

The flowers are in the true old rose style in everything but colour. They are many-petalled and open flat, a soft apricot-yellow at the centre, paling towards the petal edges. An upright, compact grower with only a slight fragrance.

Essex Poulsen, 1988
A Gold Medal winner in Dublin, this is the first in our selection of the new County series which are rapidly making a name for themselves but of which the parentages have not been released. This one has been described as like a perpetual-flowering 'Nozomi', but it is a denser grower and the flowers are of a much stronger pink and are carried in large clusters. It will make a bush 60cm (2ft) high by about 1.2m (4ft) wide, furnished with small, very glossy leaves. Try it on a bank, at the base of a hedge, or in any other position where a fair amount of ground needs to be covered quickly and profitably.

Eyeopener Ilsink, 1987. (Seedling × 'Eye Paint') × (seedling × 'Dortmund')
This is a rose that may mound up to as much as 1m (3ft) in the centre, its long shoots spreading out like a ballet skirt all round. It carries sprays of bright red, yellow-centred flowers that have been described as hydrangea-like, and I suppose they have some such resemblance, in form, if not in colour. Good, medium-green foliage.

Fair Bianca Austin, 1982
The parentage has not been given, except to say that the lovely white Gallica, 'Belle Isis', is somewhere in the lineage. Another of Austin's English roses, this time bearing comparison with the Damask rose 'Mme Hardy' as far as the flowers are concerned. They are white, packed with small petals neatly infolded and there is a green button eye. There, however, the resemblance ends, for 'Fair Bianca' makes a small, upright shrub of no more than 1m (3ft) high. Light green leaves and a strong myrrh fragrance.

Fairy Changeling Harkness, 1981. 'The Fairy' × 'Yesterday'
This makes a neat cushion about 45cm (18in) high and as much across, with fine, dark coppery leaves. The rosette-shaped flowers, freely and continuously borne, vary from rosy-pink to magenta, all colours appearing on the bush at the same time to give a most pleasing effect.

Fairy Damsel Harkness, 1981. 'The Fairy' × 'Yesterday'
The same parentage as 'Fairy Changeling' and the others in the series, showing how unpredictable rose breeding can be. This time the small rosettes are deep red against a dense background of dark green leaves, giving a most striking effect. It will reach 45cm (18in) or so in height and spread out over about 60cm (2ft).

Fairyland Harkness, 1980. 'The Fairy' × 'Yesterday'
The ideal small shrub for a mixed border as it will, with its open, informal growth, blend perfectly with other plants. The flowers are light pink and carried in dainty sprays. Will reach 60cm (2ft) in height and spread.

Fairy Prince Harkness, 1981. 'The Fairy' × 'Yesterday'
The fourth of these small shrubs from Harkness with a good deal of family resemblance and all repeat-flowering. Of them all, this is the most wide-spreading, so that it should be planted about 1.2m (4ft) apart. However, it will not get very tall, reaching probably about 75cm (2½ft) and it will be smothered throughout the season with close-set sprays of geranium-like, double flowers. Not a series of roses noted for their strong scent, but they do have a pleasing, light fragrance.

Félicité Parmentier Introduced 1836
An old garden rose of considerable charm and a member of the Alba family, which means that its leaves are of a very attractive soft grey-green. It will not usually go much above 1–1.2m (3–4ft) in height, though I have seen it rather bigger, and it bushes out well. The rounded, creamy-yellow buds (it is the only rose, old or new, that has buds of that colour), open to very double, pompon flowers of the palest pink, but still with a hint of cream about them. They are carried in small sprays over a long season, but there is no repeat. On its own roots 'Félicité Parmentier' will spread by suckers, but not quite at such a speed as the Gallica or Pimpinellifolia family.

Ferdy Suzuki, 1984. Climbing seedling × 'Petite Folie' seedling
A splendid, spreading, sprawling shrub from Japan with long, trailing shoots which will help it to make a bush 1m (3ft) high but 1.2m (4ft) wide, smothered at midsummer with clusters of small, deep salmon-pink flowers with yellow centres. Light green, rather small leaves—if only it had a better repeat performance what a rose it would be!

Fimbriata

This dates from 1891 and is something utterly different. It is possibly a cross between a Rugosa rose and a Polyantha, though in appearance it leans more towards the former. Also known as 'Phoebe's Frilled Pink' because its soft pink flowers have the petal edges serrated like a carnation or pink. The same thing can be found in the Grootendorst group of Rugosa hybrids, but here the flowers are rather larger and eventually open out flat. It makes a small bush of great refinement, about 1.5m (5ft) tall by, at most, 1.2m (4ft) across. The Royal Horticultural Society gave it an Award of Merit in 1896, but it has been largely and unjustifiably neglected since then.

Fiona Meilland, 1982. 'Sea Foam' × 'Picasso'

Bushy and spreading to 1–1.2m (3–4ft) with long, arching shoots carrying clusters of dark red flowers which pale slightly in colour towards the centre. Only moderately fragrant, they make up for this lack by being carried with the greatest freedom and more or less continuously all through the season. Smallish, dark green, glossy leaves.

Fru Dagmar Hastrup

Also known, but incorrectly, as 'Frau Dagmar Hartopp', it was raised by the Hastrup nurseries in 1914. From that time it had a long while to wait for its Award of Garden Merit from the Royal Horticultural Society in 1958, but its qualities were recognised long before that by discerning gardeners. With 'Fimbriata' (which see) it is perhaps the Rugosa most suitable for small gardens, making a shrub no more than 1.2m (4ft) tall, well covered with the usual healthy, wrinkled (rugose) leaves of the family. It also has the usual Rugosa share of prickles.

The flowers are about 9cm (3½in) across, single and pale pink, with delicate veining of the petals and creamy-yellow stamens; a most enchanting combination. They are followed by large, tomato-shaped hips of rich crimson.

Grüss an Aachen Geduldig, 1909. 'Frau Karl Druschki' × 'Franz Deegen'.

This has already been mentioned in the chapter on patio roses and could, I suppose, equally well have been described there. It has been considered by some to be the first Floribunda, but with its parents a Hybrid Perpetual and a Hybrid Tea, this hardly holds water. If anything, I suppose it could be classed as a short-growing Hybrid Tea, though its large flowers come predominantly in clusters, many-petalled in the old style, creamy-white with peach tints. It makes a compact plant about 45 × 45cm (18 × 18in) with dark green, matt foliage and is excellent for bedding as it is in flower continuously. A strong recommendation for all sorts of other uses as well.

Hampshire Kordes, 1989. Parentage not given
Another in the County series and named to celebrate the centenary of the Hampshire County Council. This is appropriate for these roses are very suitable for what is known as environmental planting, which in plain English means for planting on traffic roundabouts, between dual carriage-ways and in suchlike places. Most of the County roses have been raised by Poulsen of Denmark, but this one comes from Germany. It will make a dense, bushy shrub about 30cm (1ft) high by 60cm (2ft) wide, covered throughout the summer and autumn with clusters of glowing scarlet, single flowers with golden stamens.

Kent Poulsen, 1988. Parentage not given
Back to Denmark for the raiser of this one, which is one of the most compact. It has pure white flowers in large trusses and, for a white rose, an ability to withstand wet weather remarkably well. Dark green, healthy leaves.

La Sevillana Meilland, 1978. [('Meibrim' × 'Jolie Madame') × ('Zambra' × 'Zambra')] × [('Super Star' × 'Super Star') × ('Poppy Flash' × 'Poppy Flash')]
A rose which will make a first-rate and colourful hedge in a small garden, growing to between 1.2 and 1.5m (4 and 5ft) high and about 1m (3ft) in width, but it will also make a fine planting for a shrub border or a large tub, from which its long, lax shoots will hang down attractively, laden with clusters of semi-double, bright vermilion-red flowers. The leaves are a bronzy-red when young, developing into a pleasing dark green, against which the blooms are well displayed. There are, in addition, quite colourful hips in the autumn.
    'Pink Sevillana' is a variant in a more subdued colour.

Marjorie Fair (Red Ballerina, Red Yesterday) Harkness, 1978. 'Ballerina' × 'Baby Faurax'
Really a counterpart of 'Ballerina' (which see), but with ruby-red, white-eyed flowers. The foliage is a light, glossy green and it makes a bushy plant up to 1.2m (4ft) high and spreading out well. The winner of five international awards, which is unusual for a shrub rose.

Mary Hayley Bell Kordes, 1989. 'Zwergkonig' × seedling
This rose, with its bright pink, semi-double flowers and rather lax, informal growth, has a charm all its own, a charm which, together with other qualities more easily defined, won it the President's International Trophy and Gold Medal in the RNRS Trial in 1987. It is only moderately scented, but the light green leaves are plentiful and healthy. Count on a height of 1–1.2m (3–4ft) and a spread of about the same. It was named after the wife of the actor, Sir John Mills.

Nozomi Onedera, 1968. 'Fairy Princess' × 'Sweet Fairy'
The correct pronunciation of this Japanese rose is Noz-o-*mi* with the main emphasis on the last syllable. Classed variously as a miniature climber and as a ground-cover rose, 'Nozomi' will fill either role. It has long, arching shoots, plum-red at first and then dark green, that will drape themselves gracefully over a low wall—which is one of the nicest ways of growing it—or down a bank, and they will be spangled along their entire length with small, pearly-pink, star-like, single flowers, which will quickly fade to white in strong sunlight. Very small, dark green leaves. About 60cm × 1.8m (2 × 6ft) would be an average size.

This was the rose that set the pattern for the modern, low-growing shrubs and which proved how useful they can be in the garden. Others followed its lead and the more modern ones are probably better in many ways. However, 'Nozomi' is still distinctive and has its place.

Officinalis (*R. gallica* 'Officinalis'). The Red Rose of Lancaster; The Apothecary's Rose
Certainly the oldest rose in this book and dating back at least to the sixteenth century, but still a fine one to grow if, in a small garden, you can accommodate something that only flowers at midsummer and will almost certainly need spraying against mildew. As against this, there is a fascination in having a rose that Shakespeare probably knew and that makes up one half of the Tudor rose, the badge of England. It grows as an upright, very twiggy shrub, seldom more than 1–1.2m (3–4ft) tall with bright pink, semi-double flowers held well above the foliage, which is rather coarse in the typical Gallica style. Will spread freely by suckers if on its own roots.

Pearl Drift Le Grice, 1980. 'Mermaid' × 'New Dawn'
'Mermaid' was considered sterile and impossible to breed from until this rose arrived on the scene and, as it has not appeared in the parentage of anything since, it must be considered that the raising of 'Pearl Drift' was something of a fluke. A lucky one, certainly, for the result was a first-rate rose, about 1 × 1.2m (3 × 4ft) in size, bushy and spreading and with fine, healthy, dark green, semi-glossy leaves. The large, semi-double flowers are white, flushed pearly-pink in the bud, and are borne on sizeable trusses. A rose that deserves to be better known than it is, though there are signs that it is gradually making its presence felt.

Perle d'Or Dubreuil, 1884. *R. multiflora* seedling × 'Mme Falcot'
If the parentage usually given is correct, this would be a Tea-Polyantha, though Peter Beales suspects that it may be a sport of 'Cécile Brunner', which it resembles in many ways. It has the same almost thornless, twiggy stems and airy growth, but in the right conditions it can reach

1.8m (6ft) or even more, something I have never seen 'Cécile Brunner' achieve. Usually, however, it will not go over 1.2m (4ft), carrying flowers similar in shape and size to those of 'Cécile Brunner', though buff-yellow rather than pink. The leaves are dark green and rather pointed. A rose of great charm and delicacy.

Petite de Hollande (Pompon des Dames, Petite Junon de Hollande)
Introduced in 1800; parentage unknown
A small shrub which is probably a dwarf Centifolia in the pattern of 'De Meaux' and The Burgundian Rose. It will only grow to about 1m (3ft) and its arching canes will spread out to about the same distance. They carry 4cm (1½in) soft pink, double flowers, cupped when first they open and with a deeper colour in the centre. Lovely and sweetly scented, but only flowers at midsummer.

Pink Bells Poulsen, 1983. 'Mini-Poul' × 'Temple Bells'
One of a group of three roses, all basically similar except for their colour, the others being 'White Bells' and 'Red Bells'. They have been extensively promoted as ground-cover roses and their twiggy growth, with a dense covering of small, semi-glossy leaves, will soon form thickets under which no weed can flourish. They will reach about 1.2m (4ft) across, but as they will also mound up to at least that height, they are not the ground-hugging plants that one tends to think of in connection with ground cover. 'Pink Bells' is summer flowering only, with masses of small, double, bright pink flowers carried over a long period. This trio was bred with environmental planting in mind, and has been used widely in cities on the Continent.

Pink Drift (Kiki Rose, Caterpillar) Poulsen, 1984. 'Temple Bells' × seedling
Through 'Temple Bells', *R. wichuraiana* comes into the ancestry of this rose as it does in so many of the new ground-cover varieties. This is another Danish rose from the same raiser as the last one, carrying, mainly at midsummer, masses of small, semi-double, light pink blooms. The growth is bushy and spreading, 60cm (2ft) in height and anything up to 1–2m (3–4ft) wide. It can go further, but secateurs will control it.

Pink Meidiland (Schloss Heidegg) Meilland, 1983. 'Anne de Bretagne' × 'Nirvana'
Another rose from across the English Channel, this time from France and from a raiser who has been concentrating on ground-cover roses in recent years—with considerable success. This variety will reach about 1m (3ft) in height and spread out to about the same, making it ideal for a low, colourful hedge. Its main flush of deep pink, white-eyed flowers comes at

midsummer, and there are usually some flowers later on though not a spectacular autumn display. Upright and bushy, the plant has abundant, semi-glossy leaves and small, orange-red hips appear when the flowering is over. They make an adequate substitute for the lack of late blooms.

Pink Wave Mattock, 1983. 'Moonmaiden' × 'Eye Paint'
Soft, satiny pink, double blooms carried in great profusion on a bushy plant 60cm (2ft) tall and spreading out to 1.2m (4ft) or so. It will flower more or less non-stop for the middle three months of the summer, but there is not much to see after that.

Potter & Moore Austin, 1988
An excellent small rose combining, as with so many of David Austin's creations, the best of the old with the new. It has old-style flowers in a pleasing shade of light pink, but they are fully remontant. With its bushy, twiggy, upright growth it rather resembles the better-known 'Wife of Bath' from the same raiser (from which it was bred), but the flowers are larger and have more petals. And they are just as fragrant.

Pretty Jessica Austin, 1983. 'Wife of Bath' × unnamed seedling
This could be called the perfect 'old fashioned' rose for the small garden. Its flowers are a warm, rich pink and of the most exquisite formation, a shallow cup closely packed with petals. As a plant, it has short, compact growth and the ability to go on flowering with remarkable continuity. There is a strong fragrance and the ultimate size will be about 60 × 60cm (2 × 2ft).

Prospero Austin, 1982. 'The Knight' × 'Château de Clos Vougeot'
I have some hesitation in recommending this rose for it needs to be coddled to give of its best, which means that it is only for the real enthusiast who is prepared to humour it when it is in a temperamental mood. If this is done it will usually respond by producing the most perfect Gallica-style flowers, their numerous small petals arranged in perfect rosettes and of a rich, deep crimson, turning gradually to pleasing shades of purple and mauve. They have a strong old-rose fragrance and are carried on a plant of the ideal size for a small garden, being about 60 × 60cm (2 × 2ft).

Raubritter Kordes, 1936. 'Daisy Hill' × 'Solarium'
Not by any means a new rose and, as something rather special, it should be much more widely grown than it is. Probably the fact that it is summer-flowering only accounts partly for its absence from many nursery lists, but when in full bloom it is a sight to see, smothered in medium-sized, clear rose-pink flowers with incurving petals, which hold

their goblet shape from start to finish. They rather resemble those of the Bourbons 'La Reine Victoria' and 'Mme Pierre Oger', though perhaps not quite so double.

Up to 1m (3ft) tall, 'Raubritter' will spread out probably to twice this and is ideal for covering an old tree stump or for tumbling down a bank or over a low wall. Mildew is likely on its grey-green foliage in the second half of the summer, but with modern sprays this need not be much of a problem. This was one of the earliest roses regularly recommended for ground cover and has yet to be bettered by any non-remontant variety.

Red Bells Poulsen, 1983. 'Mini-Poul' × 'Temple Bells'
The red counterpart of 'Pink Bells', which see.

Red Blanket Ilsink, 1979. 'Yesterday' × unnamed seedling
Fully remontant and one of the earliest of the current crop of so-called ground-cover roses. It does, I feel, express its raiser's hopes and intentions rather than his achievement, for this is simply a pleasing, spreading shrub rose about 1 × 1.2m (3 × 4ft), with deep pink—almost red—semi-double flowers of medium size, very freely carried in small clusters. It is by no means a 'blanket' to smother weeds as its name would imply, but very well worth growing for what it is.

Rosa Mundi (*R. gallica* 'Versicolor')
The first record of a rose resembling this one dates from the sixteenth century. It is a written description and not a picture, which means that we cannot be sure that it is actually 'Rosa Mundi', but there is no doubt at all that this sport from 'Officinalis' (which see) is a very old rose indeed. It is reputed to be named after Fair Rosamund, the mistress of Henry II but, while this may well be true, there is no documentary evidence to take it so far back.

However that may be, it is one of the most enchanting and showy of the old roses, flowering at midsummer over a long period, its semi-double blooms opening flat and being of the palest blush-pink, splashed and striped deep pink. They are quite loosely formed and the petals attractively waved. The bush is compact and upright, 1.2 × 1m (4 × 3ft) at most, and has been used most effectively as a hedging plant in one or two of the National Trust gardens. In full bloom, these hedges are a spectacular sight, but in a small garden it must not be forgotten that they will be a long time out of flower and that Gallica foliage is not a thing of great beauty in late summer, especially when attacked by mildew. To sum up, this is a rose that really should not be missed, but in a small garden one that should be used with discretion.

Rose de Rescht
An Autumn Damask or Portland rose of great charm, said to have been
discovered in Iran and brought back to the United Kingdom by that
snapper up of unconsidered (but usually very well worthwhile) trifles,
Miss Nancy Lindsay. She wrote: 'Happened on it in a Persian garden in
ancient Resht, tribute to the tea caravans plodding Persia-wards from
China over the Central Asian steppes; it is a sturdy, yard-high bush of
glazed lizard green, perpetually emblazoned with full camellia flowers
of pigeon's blood ruby, irised with royal purple, haloed with dragon
sepals like the painted blooms on oriental faience.' I could not have put
it better myself, but had better try: a short, bushy plant with small, neat,
very full flowers of a purplish-crimson. Very fragrant and remontant.
Perhaps 1m × 60cm (3 × 2ft). My spelling of Rescht is the one usually
used nowadays, rather than the Resht of Miss Lindsay.

Rosy Cushion Ilsink, 1979. 'Yesterday' × seedling
A 1 × 1.2m (3 × 4ft) spreading shrub forming, with its dark green, glossy
foliage, a dense mound or cushion, spangled with large and small clusters
of almost single, soft pink flowers that appear first in June and carry on
right through to the autumn. Will make a fine specimen plant.

Running Maid Lens, 1985. Parentage not known
This curiously named Belgian rose has small, deep pink flowers, cupped
in shape, carried on a low-growing, spreading bush some 76cm (2½ft)
high by 1.2m (4ft) across. With those dimensions it will obviously make
good ground cover.

Rutland Poulsen, 1988. Parentage not known
One of the latest in the County series, of which several have already been
described. This one makes a small, ground-hugging plant not over 30cm
(1ft) high with glossy, dark green leaves and flowers not unlike those
of the Dog Rose, though smaller and remontant. A pretty little rose of
quiet distinction which should not be planted where harsh colours can
overwhelm it.

Scarlet Meidiland Meilland, 1987. Parentage not known
This rose will rarely exceed 1m (3ft) in height, but over a number of years
may spread out to 1.5m (5 ft) or so. It mounds up with weed-smothering
vigour and can look attractive sprawling over the edge of a path or
tumbling down a retaining wall. The 3cm (1in) very double flowers are a
bright cherry-red (rather than scarlet) and put on their main show in early
summer with only scattered blooms later. The leaves are a rich, glossy
green and cover the plant well. Some catalogues commend this rose for its
autumn blooming but this has not been notable in my experience.
Attractive, yes, but profuse, no.

Sharifa Asma Austin, 1989. Parentage not known
A short, sturdy, upright bush carrying strongly fragrant, shallowly cupped flowers in the most delicate blush-pink, which gradually reflex to form perfect pompons with the colour fading almost to white on the outer petals. Maximum height of 107cm (3½ft) is likely. Fine, healthy leaves.

Simon Robinson Robinson, 1982. *R. wichuraiana* × 'New Penny'
The kind of cross that has so often produced a new miniature rose, particularly for Ralph Moore, the American hybridist. This time, for a British raiser, it has resulted in miniature flowers of the most enchanting pink and of great delicacy. They are single and carried in small and large clusters on a spreading shrub which will not go much over 60cm (2ft) in height. Of fairly open growth, it has shiny, mid-green leaves, and the autumn blooming is particularly impressive. A real treasure.

Smarty Ilsink, 1979. 'Yesterday' × seedling
Similar in many ways to 'Rosy Cushion', this makes a vigorous, spreading, thorny bush with bright green, matt foliage and almost single, light pink blooms carried in large clusters. It is fully remontant and will reach about 90cm × 1.2m (3 × 4ft). It will make reasonably dense ground cover.

St Cecilia Austin, 1987. 'Wife of Bath' seedling
A 107cm (3½ft) by 76cm (2½ft), remontant shrub that bears a fine crop of medium-sized, cupped, creamy-buff blooms and has a good repeat in late summer. The blooms come in large, well-spaced trusses and are sweetly fragrant. One of the best of the small Austin roses.

Suffolk Kordes, 1988. Parentage not given
Bright scarlet, single flowers with golden stamens carried with great profusion over fully five months on a 45cm (18in) high shrub which will eventually reach 1m (3ft) across. A number of people appear not to like roses that show their stamens. Surely this one will convert them.

Suma Onodera, 1989
Rich, ruby-red flowers each with 30 neatly arranged petals which open out to display their stamens, the yellow of which contrasts beautifully with the rich flower colour. 'Suma' is a natural for ground cover, growing no more than 25cm (10in) high and spreading out to about 1m (3ft) all round. It will create a splendid and colourful feature if grown in a pot, on a bank, or used to underplant trees or shrubs if the shade is not too dense. Repeat-flowering, 'Suma' was bred from 'Nozomi' by the same Japanese raiser and has an excellent health record.

As already mentioned, a point to remember is that a number of these new, wide-spreading shrubs such as this one are available as standards. In general, they make much more satisfactory heads than Hybrid Teas or Floribundas which tend to have stiff, upright growth.

Surrey Kordes, 1988. 'The Fairy' × seedling
A worthy RNRS Gold Medal winner in 1987, this could be compared to a larger, and much more spreading, version of 'The Fairy'. It will not top 60cm–1m (2–3ft) but will cover a good deal of ground, bearing great swatches of soft pink, double blooms which have a deeper colour in the heart of the flower. Fully remontant, three plants of this variety would be quite sufficient to fill a bed that would take more than double that number of Floribundas. So economy is one of its virtues.

Swany Meilland, 1978. *R. sempervirens* × 'Mlle Marthe Carron'
Those who know that fine rambler 'Sander's White' will feel a comforting sense of familiarity when they see this one, though it is nothing like as vigorous. It will reach 1m (3ft) in height and have a spread of perhaps 1.5m (5ft), the growth being fairly open so that the rose can by no means be classed as a weed smotherer. The foliage is dark green and glossy, having bronze-green overtones. The very double, snow-white blooms are carried in continuous display all along the branches.

Tall Story Dickson, 1984. 'Sunsprite' × 'Yesterday'
A rather strange choice of name for a rose described in the raiser's catalogue as a 'procumbent shrub', and I have seen it going up to 1.2m (4ft) and more. Generally, however, it is more restrained and keeps to half that size with a spread rather than height of 1.2m (4ft). It has medium-sized, soft yellow flowers, which is a refreshing change when so many of these new small shrub roses are in pinks and reds. They come in clusters along the arching branches, which also bear light green, semi-glossy leaves. Recurrent flowering.

Tamora Austin, 1933. Parents not given
A reliable, free-flowering variety with fragrant, rosette-shaped blooms of a pleasing soft yellow. Bushy and upright with light green foliage, it will probably grow to 1m × 60cm (3 × 2ft) and is David Austin's own first choice of one of his roses for a small garden.

Temple Bells Morey, 1971. *R. wichuraiana* × 'Blushing Jewel'
This rose can be used more effectively as a weeping standard and in many ways resembles the better-known and rather similar 'Nozomi'. If grown as a bush it truly hugs the ground in imitation of its species parent. The small, single, white flowers appear in profusion at midsummer and

spasmodically thereafter. Perhaps there are better roses for most purposes nowadays, but this has been the parent of some of them and it still has its admirers.

White Bells Poulsen, 1983. 'Mini-Poul' × 'Temple Bells'
See 'Pink Bells' for a general description as the family resemblance is marked. With this one the very double flowers have soft yellow centres and are by no means pure white. Like 'Pink Bells' and 'Red Bells', summer-flowering only.

White Meidiland Meilland, 1986. Parentage not known
Not unlike 'Swany' but with much larger, double, white flowers, up to 10cm (4in) in diameter. It should keep to 45cm (18in) in height, but may spread out 1.2m (4ft) or so after about two years if allowed its head. This means that in a group the planting distance between bushes should be about 1m (3ft). Large, leathery, dark green, glossy leaves, plentiful enough to hide the shoots between flushes.

Wife of Bath Austin, 1969. 'Mme Caroline Testout' × ('Ma Perkins' × 'Constance Spry')
Probably the best of the early Austin English roses, a number of which had marvellous flowers but poor growth. This one is bushy and twiggy and will reach 1m × 60cm (3 × 2ft) or so, carrying medium-sized blooms, cupped in shape, sweetly scented and of a soft, warm pink. With three such fine roses as parents it should be good, and it is. It is remontant, of course.

Yellow Button Austin, 1975. Parents not given
A sturdy little bush of the Polyantha type and spreading habit. It carries double, rosette flowers in light yellow, sometimes with a darker tone in the centre of the blooms. Glossy, healthy foliage and a good fragrance. Probably 1 × 1m (3 × 3ft).

Yesterday Harkness, 1974. ('Phyllis Bide' × 'Shepherd's Delight') × 'Ballerina'
Very much a Polyantha by habit if not by breeding and a rose that makes a light, airy, freely branching bush up to 1m (3ft) or so, carrying profuse and very recurrent clusters of semi-double, deep lilac-pink blooms which pale a little towards the flower centres. The delicacy and elegance of a China rose.

CHAPTER 4

MINIATURE ROSES

I cannot tell how the truth may be;
I say the tale as 'twas said to me.

Sir Walter Scott's words could well have been written with the early history of miniature roses in mind, or for that matter the early history of roses in general. In both cases much is wrapped in mystery and likely to remain so, so that all one can do is to pick up hints and very imprecise references and build on these, a favourite pastime of rose historians over the years. Sometimes the conclusions they have drawn have later proved to be spectacularly wrong and certainly you could say that The Royal Horticultural Society lost a boot while struggling through this particular swamp. The earlier editions of their *Dictionary of Gardening* asserted that the miniature rose was in Britain in 1762, a figure that actually refers to a plate number in *Curtis's Botanical Magazine*!

Of one thing only can we be reasonably certain and that is that miniature roses originated in the Far East, for their characteristics are in the main typically those of the China rose. Whether, however, they first appeared there as a dwarf sport of an existing China rose or, as was suggested by J. Sims, writing about them in 1815, as a seedling of *R. semperflorens*, is open to doubt. Sims called the miniature *R. semperflorens minima* which, even if the parentage is correct, is not really more accurate than the more recent *R. chinensis minima*, as no wild version of the rose has ever been discovered and there seems little doubt that it originated in cultivation. This, however, did not discourage people from giving the miniature rose other pseudo-botanical names such as *R. indica humilis* and even *R. lawranceana* as a tribute to Mary Lawrance whose outstanding contribution to rose literature, *A Collection of Roses From Nature*, had been published in 1799. An illustration in *Curtis's Botanical Magazine* shows *R. lawranceana* as having single, blush-pink flowers.

The botanist John Lindley, writing in 1820, quotes Robert Sweet as saying that the miniature came from China via Mauritius, which was on one of the trade routes from the Far East. He gives a precise date, 1810, but all the other evidence, sketchy though it may be, indicates that this should be taken only as approximate. All one can safely say, I think, is that miniatures arrived in England very early in the nineteenth century, from where they were introduced to France by Louis Noisette, the man whose name was to be immortalised (as Nancy Lindsay might have put it) in the Noisette climbers.

As novelties the miniature roses became immensely popular, particularly on the French side of the Channel. They were the fashionable plant to have, grown in pots in conservatories or for the decoration of the salons of the aristocracy. They were not the easiest of roses to breed from as they did not set seed very readily, but by 1829 there were certainly varieties in white, red, crimson and in various shades of pink. We know this from descriptions of some of them in a book called *The Flower Garden* by M'Intosh, gardener to the King of the Belgians. 'Lilliputienne', 'Fairy', 'Caprice de Dames' and 'Gloire de Lawrance' are some of those he mentions, which brings in Mary Lawrance's name once more. From the frequency with which she is associated with miniature roses it would seem that she must have played a significant part in their development, but there is no evidence that this was so.

It was clearly not realised in their early days in the West that miniature roses would make very successful garden plants and that they could be grown permanently out of doors. If this had been tried, their story would probably have been very different and they would have become a permanent part of the gardening scene much earlier than they did. As it was, once their appeal as novelties began to wane, first in England and then rather later in France, they gradually dropped almost completely from sight. It was only through a stroke of luck that they did not vanish altogether.

In 1918 a tiny, pale pink rose was discovered by a Major Roulet growing in a pot on the window sill of a house in the village of Onnens in Switzerland. According to the owners of the house it had come originally from France, and had been in the village for something close on a hundred years. There was no reason to doubt that at least the first part of this statement was true, and Major Roulet was allowed to show the rose to a Monsieur Correvon, a nurseryman friend of his in Geneva. The latter realised at once that the rose had possibilities and, writing in the *Gardeners' Chronicle* in 1922, M. Correvon told how he had just seen the Roulet miniature in his garden in full bud under a covering of snow, the first time as far as is known that its suitability for outdoor use was demonstrated. Correvon called the rose *R. rouletii* in honour of his friend, which would seem to have been rather hard on the anonymous Onnens family who had cared for it for something not far short of a century and without whom it would probably have ceased to exist.

So, under yet another botanically invalid name, the miniature rose began to flourish once more, though a certain amount of confusion about its identity once more comes into the story. Some people hold that *R. rouletii* is identical to the French rose called 'Pompon de Paris', which appears to have been known in the nineteenth century. As 'Pompon de Paris' is still going strong today, though usually sold only in its climbing form, it presumably must have survived the decline of the miniatures as its date of introduction is given as 1839. The rose breeders' bible, *Modern Roses*, says that 'Pompon de Paris' was formerly sold as a pot plant in Paris markets and describes its pink colouring as being deeper than that of *R. rouletii*, with which I would agree, and if it is not the same rose, where was it during the years of the latter's eclipse? On another window sill? And why was it the discovery of *R. rouletii* (which at best should be called *R.* 'Rouletii'), that brought about the revival of the fortunes of the miniature rose rather than the much more attractive 'Pompon de Paris'?

However that may be, Major Roulet's discovery did not immediately take the fashionable world by storm. The advance of the miniatures was this time much more gradual and for the first time a serious breeding programme was undertaken. In their earlier days plant breeding had been a very hit and miss affair and not properly understood by most nurserymen. By the time the miniature returned, however, there had been a radical change. Instead of growing two roses side by side and hoping for the best, as had been the practice for years, they would be cross-pollinated by hand.

The first of the hybridists to show real progress with miniatures was Jan de Vink Boskoop in Holland. He crossed *R. rouletii* with a dwarf Polyantha rose, 'Gloria Mundi', and this produced, in 1930, a crimson-flowered seedling even smaller than *R. rouletii*, which de Vink named 'Peon'. This name was changed to 'Tom Thumb' when the rose was introduced to America in 1936, and the Americans really took it to their hearts. So much so, indeed, that stock ran out before advance orders could be fulfilled and sales had to be suspended until 1938 so that supplies could be built up.

'Peon' proved to be a good parent of other roses and altogether de Vink raised seven varieties that made their mark. These included one which still heads popularity lists today, the pearly-pink 'Cinderella', and 'Humpty Dumpty'.

Another nurseryman prominent in the early history of miniature breeding was the Spaniard Pedro Dot, who was the first to use Hybrid Teas as well as Polyanthas in his crosses. He was encouraged to do this when he came to realise that the miniature rose gene is the dominant one in any cross, so that small size is retained in the progeny. 'Perla de Alcanada' ('Baby Crimson'), 'Perla de Montserrat' and 'Estrellita de Oro' ('Baby Gold Star') were some of his varieties, the latter, brought out in 1940, being the first yellow miniature. It had the Hybrid Tea 'Eduardo

Toda' as one parent and *R. rouletii* as the other and is still to be found on many nursery lists today. However, Pedro Dot's own favourite was a variety called 'Si', which means 'yes'. This was, he explained, because of the number of times he had to answer 'si' when he was asked if a plant so small could really be a rose. All told, he produced some ten successful varieties before his death in 1976.

Quite a few other European breeders have been successful with miniatures, though it was not until comparatively recent times that they showed much interest in them. An exception to this was, perhaps, Meilland of France, who put some fine varieties on the market such as 'Colibri', 'Starina' and 'Darling Flame', while Sam McGredy, before he took off for New Zealand, came up with 'Wee Man', launched with something of a flourish after gaining a Certificate of Merit in the RNRS Trials but proving in the garden to be susceptible to black spot. Later, it was McGredy who produced the first ground-cover miniature in 'Snow Carpet'.

Tantau's 'Baby Masquerade' from Germany has probably been the most widely planted miniature of all time and has the Floribunda 'Masquerade' as one parent. Its flowers, leaves and shoots are all suitably small for a miniature, but it does grow very tall—up to 60cm (2ft) in a place that suits it—though the average is rather less than this.

'Tom Thumb' went from Europe to America and started a trend, but the United States did not for long depend on imports from abroad. Dr Dennison Morey and a number of others produced some interesting varieties, but it is Ralph S. Moore of the Sequoia Nursery in California who stands head and shoulders above the rest, not only in his native country, but world-wide. Working with great patience and persistence for something like thirty years, he has now a truly awe-inspiring collection of offspring behind him and it would seem that there are many more to come. One could list his varieties by the hundred and it is probably safe to say that in any random list of miniature roses on sale anywhere in the world, four out of five would be from the Moore stable. Largely due to his work, there are now nurseries in the United States that sell nothing else, and his varieties that have gone overseas have helped in no small measure to make the miniature's merits for small-scale gardening appreciated to the full. Only one small cloud has appeared on the horizon in that British nurserymen have not always been as discriminating as they might have been in choosing Moore varieties that will thrive in the climate of the United Kingdom. There are some which should never have crossed the Atlantic, successful though they may have been in their own country.

Moore used a cross between the rambler *R. wichuraiana* and a German Floribunda called 'Floradora' as the basis of his early breeding, and a pink miniature climber of his own raising called 'Zee' was also an important factor in his subsequent work. He was responsible for the introduction of mauve-coloured miniatures and also some with pink and white striping such as 'Stars 'n' Stripes', but perhaps his greatest breeding achievement has been with Moss roses. These had for long been considered virtually sterile, an increase in varieties coming about only through the family's propensity to sport. Moore, however, succeeded in bringing Moss roses into his breeding lines, and his rose-red 'Fairy Moss' was introduced in 1969. Better still was 'Dresden Doll', which reached the European markets in 1975, though it is perhaps rather too big to qualify as a true miniature.

It makes a substantial bush up to 45cm (18in) tall, and its cupped, pink flowers with their mossy flower stalks and sepals are about 4cm (1½in) in diameter, which brings us, as one might say, to the other end of the problem breeders have been creating for gardeners and which was touched on in the chapter on patio roses. There it was largely a question of Polyantha roses getting larger and larger until they began to merge into the Hybrid Teas. Here it is a question of very much the same problem arising with the miniatures.

In the early days all of them were either white, red, crimson, or in various shades of pink. However, neither the public nor the rose breeders were content with this and, in order to widen the colour range, they were increasingly crossed with either Hybrid Teas or Floribundas. The dominant miniature gene and its effect on size has already been mentioned, but despite this the flowers and the bushes on which they grew did gradually get marginally bigger until at length they came face to face with Floribundas which were getting smaller—and the patio rose was born.

In their early days, as has been said, miniature roses were grown almost exclusively in pots and used for indoor display. Nowadays so many of them are raised commercially from cuttings or else micro-propagated, rather than sold as bare-root plants budded on to understocks, they tend to appear in nurseries and garden centres in pots, and this has resulted in many people considering them to be houseplants pure and simple. Their tiny size and sometimes rather fragile appearance has led to the belief that they are far from robust. A touch of frost and they would fade away. Nothing, however, could be further from the truth.

With a good deal of help, and providing that fairly exacting conditions are fulfilled, it is true that miniatures can be grown indoors. What these conditions are will be described shortly, but without them no miniature would survive in the dry atmosphere of a modern house. The leaves would simply turn yellow and drop off it they were kept in a centrally heated building over a long period, but they can be brought indoors when the buds are just beginning to show colour, provided that they are taken out again and put in the garden or greenhouse when flowering is done. While in the house they should be stood on a tray of fine gravel with water up to the level of the bases of the pots and placed where they can get as much light as possible. Not, however, where the full heat of the sun can beat down on them through a window.

If, however, you are prepared to take the trouble, you can prolong their stay indoors indefinitely and have the little bushes flowering in the winter months. For this a small alcove in a room without excessive artificial heating is an ideal place and a temperature of 21–24°C (70–75°F) should be aimed for, together with the gravel tray to provide humidity. In this alcove the roses can stand on a table with two 40-watt fluorescent lighting tubes mounted 25–30cm (10–12in) above the plants. These should be switched on for twelve hours a day on average, and as a refinement a small electric fan can be mounted about 1.5m (5ft) away to create a moving stream of air that will keep mildew at bay. A white-painted wall behind the roses and possibly a reflective surface above the fluorescent tubes will ensure that there is sufficient light, but quite frankly I would doubt that so much trouble is worth while when there are many good houseplants which thrive with the minimum of attention.

For growing miniatures out of doors a very different picture emerges, for most of them are perfectly hardy in the United Kingdom. Just the same it must be recognised that, to give of their best, they do need looking after and to be fed, sprayed and pruned just as larger kinds of roses have to be. There is sometimes a tendency just to plant miniatures and then leave them to get on with it. A few can cope with this, but most will end up looking rather sorry for themselves, a number, for instance, being rather prone to die-back. At their best, however, all of them can look enchanting and it is very well worth while taking a little trouble with them.

Miniature roses can be used for edging rosebeds, provided that the other roses in the beds are not so tall as to leave them permanently in the shade. As has been stressed elsewhere, all roses are sun-lovers, and miniatures are no exception. They can also be used most successfully for bordering paths and the taller ones will come into their own for lining drives or surrounding a gravel forecourt. In situations such as this it is probably best to use one variety so as to achieve a reasonable uniformity in height and bushiness. Miniature varieties vary quite markedly in their habit of growth and, while mixed colours can be attractive, for a path, especially a narrow one, a certain amount of regimentation is not out of order. At any rate avoid a sprawling variety such as 'Pink Tips'. Some edging plants one can tread on and they will come up smiling, but roses are not among them.

Making a complete miniature rose garden is sometimes put forward as a good way of growing these little roses, but I have never seen it carried out with complete success. For some reason the scale is never just right, though it is difficult to say exactly why this should be. Possibly the reason is that it is usually tried in too small a space. Miniature roses are, on average, about one-quarter to one-third the size of Hybrid Teas or Floribundas and it is very rare for this difference to be reflected in the size of miniature beds. The result is that the roses look too big, especially if they are varieties—and there are quite a few—which already have flowers which look too big for the individual plants.

Then there is the question of paths between the beds. If they are to be of grass, they should ideally be no more than about 23cm (9in) wide, so how do you cut them? And unless a bowling green smoothness is achieved, the grass itself will be out of scale. The answer is small paving stones or fine stone chippings, but all-in-all, while attractive in theory, a complete miniature rose garden needs, to get it right in the first place and to keep it looking neat afterwards, a formidable amount of work.

So far we have only discussed growing miniature roses out of doors at ground level, which has the disadvantage for most people of middle age and beyond, that the beauty of the individual blooms passes them by. Bending becomes less easy as the years go past and some of the miniatures are scented as well as being good to look at close to, and this can only be appreciated if they are cut for the house or else grown more nearly at eye level. Fortunately this is not difficult to do.

They can, for instance, be grown on rockeries—preferably in small clumps rather than singly—and so provide late colour for a garden feature in which it is usually confined to spring. The upright stance of the bushes, which will, of course, provide early colour as well, makes a useful contrast to the low, creeping habit of many of the alpines, and a rock

8 Miniature roses in a terraced bed

9 Miniature roses in a planting trough, on top of a low brick wall

garden should give the good drainage the roses need. It is important, however, to make sure that they have a good, unrestricted root-run, which the stones will keep cool and moist.

Another attractive way of getting miniatures growing well above ground level is to incorporate a planting trough in the top of a brick or stone wall which runs alongside a path. The trough should be at least 20cm (8in) deep and 15cm (6in) wide, and the same kind of wall can be built to surround a sunken garden. Even better is to surround it with terraced beds with brick retaining walls, each level of the terracing planted with miniature roses. One variety per level can be chosen or they can be set out in blocks of eight or nine each of a number of varieties, provided always that thought is given to colour harmony.

Each terrace should be about 30cm (1ft) above the one below it, and miniature standard roses can be grown in the top bed to add variety. A rose such as 'Nozomi', with its white, star-like flowers, can be used to trail down over the lower retaining wall, but it is best not to try to incorporate climbing miniatures in such a scheme. They are usually far too vigorous, 'Climbing Pompon de Paris', for instance, reaching the eaves of a house with considerable ease.

Few amateurs have succeeded in breeding new miniature roses, but a notable exception came when Chris Warner won the Royal National Rose Society's top award, The President's International Trophy and Gold Medal, with his 'Chewizz', a miniature climber of very bushy habit which will go up to 2.1–2.4m (7–8ft) and will be covered from top to bottom with deep green foliage and carry orange-red, semi-double flowers from mid-June till the end of October.

This, however, was an exception, as it is very difficult to get miniatures to set seed. However, they can be increased very easily from cuttings, though this does not, of course, produce new varieties. It will produce instead with the greatest of ease limitless new plants of existing varieties, which makes it an attractive proposition for the commercial grower as well as the amateur. While with larger roses cuttings will usually take three years or even more to develop into full-sized plants, with miniatures this time can be halved. The resulting plants will, too, be smaller than those that have been budded on to rootstock, which in a miniature is a good thing. Budding can convert what would on its own roots be a very average-sized miniature into a patio rose.

What might be regarded as an unfortunate development in the culture of miniature roses has come with mass production. Commercially it makes sense, but it does bring us nearer to the disposable rose, a rose that is only kept for the period of its flowering and then thrown away. Not that this is a completely new development in the flower trade, but it is new with roses and as such to be regretted by anyone who loves them. The process involves cuttings being taken and grown under glass in highly artificial conditions so that they can be on sale eleven weeks later. The actual cuttings are taken mechanically and the plants are only touched by human hands twice before reaching the point of sale. Micropropagation is also playing its part, producing thousands of miniature roses, mostly nameless varieties, that appear on supermarket shelves among the houseplants.

It has already been said that miniatures need just as much looking after as any other kind of rose. They are just as likely to succumb to mildew and black spot, die-back and insect invasion as their larger counterparts; some people hold that they are more so, but I think that the problem may be this. Walking along a bed of roses of normal height it is quite easy to see the first signs of mildew or black spot or to notice an invasion of greenfly or caterpillars. One scarcely has to bend down to see what is happening, but with miniatures at ground level disease may be able to get a firm hold before it is really noticed. The first signs that anything is amiss might well be the beginnings of defoliation; too late to do anything. For this reason it is probably as well to carry out preventive spraying of miniatures, though for other roses I am a firm believer in spraying only when disease is actually seen.

Varieties of miniature roses

Air France (Rosy Meillandina, American Independence) Meilland, 1982. 'Minijet' × ('Darling Flame' × 'Perla de Montserrat')
Bushy and upright to about 30cm (12in) with plentiful dark green leaves. Medium-sized, double blooms in clear rose-pink, carried in large clusters and opening wide to show an attractive boss of yellow stamens. Healthy.

Angela Rippon (Ocaru, Ocarina) De Ruiter, 1978. 'Rosy Jewel' × 'Zorina'
This makes a vigorous, bushy plant reaching about 30cm (12in) and carrying fine sprays of large, double blooms in coral-pink. A useful one for the show bench because of the quality of its fragrant blooms but, because of its overall size, sometimes to be found listed among the patio roses.

Anna Ford Harkness 1980. 'Southampton' × 'Darling Flame'
Another rose sometimes classed among the patio varieties and one of such quality that it won the President's International Trophy, the top award in the RNRS Trials, in 1981, a most unusual distinction for a miniature. It makes a plant with fine, glossy foliage and will reach 45cm (18in) in height. It is, however, freely branching and makes a bushy plant. The flowers are very showy, being semi-double and bright orange-red with yellow centres. They are carried in good clusters over a long period and repeat well. A generally very healthy rose.

Apricot Sunblaze (Savamark, Mark One) Saville, 1984. 'Sheri Anne' × 'Glenfiddich'
A neat but rather thorny bush that will reach 38cm (15in) and will carry throughout the summer and autumn an almost non-stop crop of bright, orange-red blooms in small, compact clusters. Glossy foliage and a good scent.

Baby Darling Moore, 1964. 'Little Darling' × 'Magic Wand'
This is a very attractive little rose if you are prepared to give it some winter protection, especially in the northern counties of the United Kingdom. The large, double blooms are in blends of orange and pink and come in medium-sized clusters on a bushy plant about 30cm (12in) tall. The flowers last well when cut and, though quite an old variety, still one that picks up points on the show bench.

Baby Faurax Lille, 1924. Unknown parentage, but possibly a dwarf sport of a Multiflora rambler
A rarely seen rose, which may be found in catalogues listed as a Polyantha. Hybridist Jack Harkness describes it as the nearest thing there is to a blue rose, and he has used it quite extensively in his breeding programmes. It is not, however, the most robust of growers, but its very attractive double flowers make it worth trying in a pot in the greenhouse.

Baby Gold Star (Estrellita de Oro) Dot, 1940. 'Eduardo Toda' × R. 'Rouletii'
One of the classic miniatures that goes on and on with its popularity

seemingly undiminished. Large, semi-double, deep yellow flowers come with great freedom on a plant of rather open, spreading growth and which may reach 30cm (12in) in height. The colour is likely to fade in hot sun and the mid-green leaves are likely to be attacked by black spot most summers, but neither of these faults seems to knock it off its pedestal.

Baby Masquerade (Baby Carnaval) Tantau, 1956. 'Peon' × 'Masquerade' Another classic with which the only fault I can find is that it has a reluctance to shed its petals once the flowers are over. A hand brushed over the top of the bush (which is not very thorny) will get rid of most of them, but just the same regular dead-heading is advised. A tall grower, to 45cm (18in) or so, with clusters of semi-double blooms, opening yellow and turning red, which deepens as they age. The leaves are small, dark green and plentiful. A very twiggy grower, a few of the shoots dying back each year and so needing to be removed at pruning time.

Baby Sunrise McGredy, 1984. 'Benson & Hedges Special' × 'Moana' Shapely blooms of coppery-apricot, semi-double and borne in good-sized clusters. Semi-glossy leaves and a bushy plant which will grow to 30cm (1ft).

Bambino Dot, 1953
A pink sport of 'Perla de Alcanada', which it resembles in all other ways.

Benson & Hedges Special (Dorola) McGredy, 1982. 'Darling Flame' × 'Marbella'
A Certificate of Merit winner and first-rate rose in deep, clear yellow. The flowers are shapely and produced in good-sized clusters on a bush which will reach 30cm (1ft), and has dark green, semi-glossy leaves. There is a slight fragrance.

Bit o' Sunshine Moore, 1956. 'Copper Glow' × 'Zee'
This has remained popular for many years despite a proneness to disease and the fact that the bright yellow, double flowers are really too big for the size of the plant. At its best it will reach 30cm (1ft). The growth is upright and the leaves mid-green and semi-glossy.

Blue Peter (Azulabria, Bluenette) De Ruiter, 1982. 'Little Flirt' × seedling
Upright and reasonably well branched to 30cm (1ft) or so, with small, light green, semi-glossy foliage. The double, lilac-purple blooms are carried in medium-sized clusters. One of the best of the so-called 'blue' miniatures, none of which is, of course, a true blue.

Bobolink Moore, 1959. (*R. wichuraiana* × 'Floradora') × ('Oakington Ruby' × 'Floradora')
The rose-pink petals of this one pale to white in the heart of the very double flowers. They are slightly fragrant and carried on a tall, bushy grower that will reach 38cm (15in).

Born Free Moore, 1978. 'Red Pinocchio' × 'Little Chief'
Very spectacular, especially if several bushes are grouped together, for the blooms are a brilliant orange-scarlet, opening wide to show yellow stamens. They hold their colour well, even in strong sunlight, and over a long period. It makes an upright, bushy plant, not particularly tall at 23cm (9in) or so.

Bush Baby Pearce, 1986. Parentage not given
A real baby or true miniature as it will only reach about 15cm (6in) in height. It is a dense, leafy grower, very healthy, and has delicate, pale salmon-pink blooms.

Chelsea Pensioner Mattock, 1982. Parentage not given
Upright in growth and eventually reaching about 45cm (18in), this is one that could just be squeezed into the patio rose category. The foliage is a pleasing grey-green and the very double blooms, which come with considerable freedom and good continuity, are deep scarlet, shading to gold at the base.

Cinderella De Vink, 1952. 'Cécile Brunner' × 'Peon'
For a rose to remain in our affections for almost forty years it must have something special and, as indicated in the opening section of this chapter, this one has—the most enchanting, tiny, Hybrid Tea-type blooms which are white with just a hint of pink. A little more fragrance and they would be perfect. The bush is sturdy and almost thornless, with light green foliage. It should reach 25cm (10in) or so in height.

Colibri Meilland, 1958. 'Goldilocks' × 'Perla de Montserrat'
The double flowers of this one are buff-yellow, flushed orange and are carried in medium-sized clusters. Upright and bushy to 30cm (1ft) and with dark green, glossy foliage which shows up the blooms particularly well. A good and popular rose that has deservedly stood the test of time.

Colibri '79 Meilland, 1979. Parentage not stated
Some confusion here because this rose, in addition to having virtually the same name as the previous one, is now included in the Meilland 'Sunblaze' series, which has already absorbed and changed the names of other roses, such as 'Rise 'n' Shine', which appears sometimes as 'Golden

Sunblaze'. All rather unnecessary, but what appear to be marketing considerations should not be allowed to detract from what is a very good little rose with yellow flowers, heavily flushed pink and orange. Bushy to about 25cm (10in).

Coralin (Carolin, Carolyn, Perla Corail) Dot, 1955. 'Méphisto' × 'Perla de Alcanada'
The large, full blooms vary in colour from coral-pink almost to red, and are carried in good-sized clusters on a medium to tall bush that at best will reach 38cm (15in). Mid-green, semi-glossy leaves and a whiff of scent from the flowers.

Cricri (Gavolda) Meilland, 1958. ('Alain' × 'Independence') × 'Perla de Alcanada'
A rose that seems to be gradually fading from the minds of growers and hence the nursery lists for no discernible reason, for it is still just as good as ever it was. The clusters of small, fully double, rosette-shaped flowers are of a soft salmon-pink and are carried on an upright plant, some 30cm (1ft) in height, which has leathery, mid-green foliage.

Crimson Gem (Flammette) De Ruiter, 1974. 'Lillan' × a Polyantha seedling
Ovoid buds open to medium-sized, very double, cupped, slightly fragrant, deep red flowers carried in good trusses. Bronzy, rather soft foliage on a taller than average plant which can be expected to reach 45cm (18in). Very floriferous.

Darling Flame Meilland, 1971. ('Rimosa' × 'Rosina') × 'Zambra'
Its brilliant orange-vermilion flowers have made this one of the most popular of miniatures and, as they are good for cutting and last well in water, it is a top show rose, too. It is a compact grower reaching about 45cm (18in) with dark green, glossy foliage which, in the climate of the United Kingdom at least, will need spraying to keep disease at bay.

Dollie B Robinson, 1983. Parentage not given
Large flowers in velvety red with a silver reverse. Bushy to 30cm (1ft) and carrying dark, glossy leaves. This one is beginning to make its name on the show bench.

Double Joy Moore, 1979. Parentage not known.
Double, 4cm (1½in) pink blooms like those of a Hybrid Tea, and fragrant to boot, give this rose a special appeal. They make good cut flowers so the rose is likely to have a future on the show bench when, as is gradually happening, it becomes better known. Backing the flowers are plentiful matt, green leaves and the bush is in the 25–38cm (10–15in) range.

Dresden Doll Moore, 1975. 'Fairy Moss' × unnamed Moss rose seedling
Not the first Moss rose miniature to come from this famous American breeder, but the first to make an impact outside his native country. As has already been recorded, Moore's work proved that the Moss rose family, though reluctant to co-operate, could be used in breeding and this is a sample of the results coming from his long and patient work with this group.

'Dresden Doll' is really large enough to be included among the patio roses, but was introduced as a miniature before the former were thought of as a separate class. It will reach 30–45cm (12–18in) and is of spreading habit, well branched and carrying its large, cupped, semi-double, shell-pink flowers in large clusters. They emerge from heavily mossed buds. May need watching for mildew.

Duke Sunblaze Meilland, 1986. Parentage not given
A strong-growing bush, with pink, semi-double flowers that will reach a height of 25cm (10in).

Dwarfking (Zwergkonig) Kordes, 1957. 'World Fair' × 'Peon'
One of the early miniatures which remained at the top of the popularity charts for many years. Now, though perhaps superseded by other varieties, it still has its place in any representative collection. It makes an upright rather slender plant with small clusters of semi-double, cupped, reddish-carmine blooms. It should reach 30cm (1ft).

Easter Morning Moore, 1960. 'Golden Glow' × 'Zee'
The ivory-white blooms are large and very double, shapely at first in the best Hybrid Tea tradition, but opening wide to show their stamens. For a rose with upwards of 60 petals in each flower, they are surprisingly resistant to rain, and if only they were carried with rather more freedom this would come close to being an ideal miniature. It is a bushy grower, to 30cm (1ft) in height, with glossy, dark green leaves. Despite my slight reservation, there is really no better white rose of its type.

Eleanor Moore, 1960. (*R. wichuraiana* × 'Floradora') × (seedling × 'Zee')
A miniature which, like 'Dwarfking', is perhaps past its prime but can still rest on its very considerable laurels and match up to many a later introduction. The coral-pink of the flowers tends to deepen with age so that there is, overall, a two-toned effect. They come in large clusters on a bushy, upright plant with glossy foliage. Up to 30cm (1ft) in height.

Elfin Poulsen, 1896. Parentage not known
A rose that is just beginning to make an impact in the United Kingdom,

where its good qualities took some time to be recognised. It has large trusses of semi-double, deep pink flowers that appear in some lights to have a bluish tinge; a most pleasing and unusual effect. They are carried on a low-growing, compact plant, to 25cm (10in) in height, with mid-green, glossy foliage. Extremely free-flowering.

Fashion Flame Moore, 1977. 'Little Darling' × 'Fire Princess'
Peachy-red to orange in colour, this showy rose has fairly large, double blooms carried on a robust, bushy plant which will achieve 25cm (10in) or so. Will need some winter protection in the United Kingdom, but worth taking some trouble with, especially if you are a rose exhibitor.

Fire Princess Moore, 1969. 'Baccara' × 'Eleanor'
Medium-sized, scarlet blooms which make good cut flowers as the stems are long and almost thornless. Growth is upright and tall to 30cm (1ft). A fairly open-growing plant with mid-green, glossy leaves.

Firefly McGredy, 1988. Parentage not given
Not to be confused with two other roses which have borne this name, one a Floribunda introduced as recently as 1975, though it does not seem to have remained in the nursery lists. A glowing orange-bronze distinguishes the flowers of this rose, which is a tall, well branched grower making a 45cm (18in) plant.

Ginny-Lou Robinson, 1984. Parentage not given
The second rose in our list from a raiser who is just beginning to make his mark with some first-rate varieties, yet to attract the attention—and distribution—they deserve. This one has blooms in a glowing pink with petals pointed to give a star-like effect. The red-tinted young growth matures to a dark, glossy green. Height 25cm (10in).

Gold Coin Moore, 1967. 'Golden Glow' × 'Magic Wand'
Semi-double flowers in a rich, buttercup yellow on a well branched, bushy plant that is likely to suffer from a certain amount of die-back in hard winters. Mid-green leaves; will make 25cm (10in) in height.

Gold Pin Mattock, 1974. Parentage not given
Growth bushy but not over-vigorous and protection from disease on the bronzy foliage may be needed. Nevertheless, a cheerful little rose at its best and very free with its semi-double, slightly fragrant, deep golden-yellow flowers. Probably 25cm (10in).

Golden Angel Moore, 1975. 'Golden Glow' × ('Little Darling' × seedling)

A sturdy grower and probably about the most robust of the yellow miniatures, which do not on the whole seem to relish the climate of the United Kingdom—something which could, of course, have been said about yellow roses in general not so many years back. This variety has scented, bright yellow, very double flowers which emerge from tiny, rounded buds and which last for a very long time, both on the bush and when cut. The maximum height is about 25cm (10in).

Golden Sunblaze
See 'Rise 'n' Shine'.

Green Diamond Moore, 1975. Polyantha × 'Sheri Anne'
A curiosity rather than a beauty, which has tiny, greenish-pink, fully double flowers, borne in clusters and which open very slowly, after which the pink tinge vanishes. Not a rose to make a show in the garden but one about which it is usual to say that flower arrangers will love it. It will grow to 25cm (10in) and has mid-green, leathery foliage.

Gypsy Jewel Moore, 1975. 'Little Darling' × 'Little Buckaroo'
A very pleasing rose, tall for a miniature at 45cm (18in) and rather open and spreading in growth. It carries its deep rose-pink, double blooms in small clusters and the foliage is dark green and glossy.

Hakuun Poulsen, 1962. Seedling × ('Pinocchio' × 'Pinocchio')
A miniature or a patio rose? You can take your choice with this one but, whichever class you put it in, it is a more than worthy representative, never out of flower right through the season. Very sturdy and 45cm (18in) high, it bears fine trusses of buff-orange flowers which soon fade to an attractive creamy-white. A rose, the sheer flower-power of which must thrust it to the forefront of attention before long.

Happy Hour Saville, 1983. ('Tamango' × 'Yellow Jewel') × 'Zinger'
Very large clusters of semi-double, bright red flowers with yellow centres on a bushy, spreading plant with dark green, glossy leaves and growing to about 30cm (1ft) high.

Happy Thoughts Moore, 1978. (*R. wichuraiana* × 'Floradora') × 'Sheri Anne'
Blends of pink, coral and yellow distinguish this rose's flowers. They are fully double and carried in good-sized clusters. The leaves are mid-green and glossy. Height to 25cm (10in).

Heidi Christensen, 1978. 'Fairy Moss' × 'Iceberg'
Constantly in flower, this little rose, only 20cm (8in) tall, has small,

double, very fragrant flowers of clear pink. Vigorous and bushy, with first-rate, glossy foliage. Do not expect moss, though, despite the parentage.

Hollie Roffey Harkness, 1986. Parentage not given
The first miniature raised by Jack Harkness, one of the UK's leading hybridists, and nobody could say that he had made a bad start, even though the rose has not made much of an impact on the public. The rose-pink double flowers, about 3cm (1in) across, are packed with about 60 petals each, forming the most charming rosettes. Dark, polished leaves on a 30cm (1ft), spreading, bushy plant complete the picture.

Hombre Jolly, 1982. 'Humdinger' × 'Rise 'n' Shine'
Bushy and reaching no more than 25cm (10in), this makes a sturdy plant bearing double, well-formed blooms, deep apricot-orange but fading, and with the petal tips rather pointed after the fashion of a dahlia.

Hula Girl Williams, 1975. 'Miss Hillcrest' × 'Mabel Dot'
Orange-salmon blooms well displayed on a tall, 38cm (15in) bush. They are large and full and carried in small clusters.

Janice Tellian Moore, 1979. 'Fairy Moss' × 'Fire Princess'
Rosette blooms with a multitude of tiny, pointed petals in soft pink, giving a most charming effect. It makes a small, compact bush, to 25cm (10in) with mid-green, semi-glossy leaves and is rapidly gaining a name as an exhibition variety. This means, of course, that it lasts well in water in the exhibition tent, and in the house, too.

Jennie Robinson Robinson, 1983. Parentage not given
Dark, glossy leaves show off well the yellow and red bicolour blooms of this attractive little rose. As with many other bicolours, the bright colours fade to pink after a while, but they do so attractively and do not lose their charm (or their fragrance). Some 38cm (15in) is the ultimate height that should be expected.

Judy Fischer Moore, 1968. 'Little Darling' × 'Magic Wand'
One of the best roses from the Moore stables, which has stood the test of time. Shapely, double, deep pink flowers on an average-sized bush with dark green, bronze-tinted leaves. Free-flowering and a quite unfading colour in the strongest sunlight. To 38cm (15in) tall.

June Time Moore, 1963. (*R. wichuraiana* × 'Floradora') × [('Etoile Luisante' seedling × 'Red Ripples') × 'Zee']
Small blooms with up to 75 petals in light pink with a darker reverse. The

bush is unlikely to top 25cm (10in), but is a robust, bushy grower with glossy foliage. Constantly in flower.

Lavender Jewel Moore, 1978. 'Little Chief' × 'Angel Face'
Shapely, high-centred flowers with 40 petals in lavender-mauve. The growth is rather lax but the plant should reach 38cm (15in) and carries dark green, semi-glossy leaves.

Lavender Lace Moore, 1968. 'Ellen Poulsen' × 'Debbie'
Lavender-pink flowers, small, double and high-centred on a very bushy grower that will not top 23cm (9in), which to my mind is what a miniature rose should be. Plentiful, small, glossy leaves.

Lemon Delight Moore, 1978. 'Fairy Moss' × 'Gold Moss'
Our second Moss rose from Ralph Moore, this time with semi-double, clear lemon-yellow flowers coming from well-mossed, pointed buds. Bushy and upright with abundant bloom. Mid-green leaves. 45cm (18in).

Little Artist (Top Gear) McGredy, 1986. 'Eye Paint' × 'Ko's Yellow'
One of Sam McGredy's 'hand-painted' roses and the first miniature to have its petals patterned in this fashion. The semi-double blooms are a mixture of crimson and white, an unusual combination in this class of rose, and have a strong fragrance. An RNRS certificate of Merit winner, this makes a bushy, eyecatching plant about 30cm (1ft) tall. The flowers are excellent for cutting.

Little Buckaroo Moore, 1956. (*R. wichuraiana* × 'Floradora') × ('Oakington Ruby' × 'Floradora')
A rose that has been on many nursery lists for a long time and only recently has there been anything to rival it in its colour range. 'Magic Carrousel' is very similar but they are not identical, for 'Little Buckaroo' has more red on the petal edges and a smaller white centre to the flowers, which are delicately scented. Growth is spreading and the leaves glossy and bronze-tinted. 25cm (10in).

Little Breeze McCann, 1981. 'Anytime' × 'Elizabeth of Glamis'
Semi-double, orange-red flowers which fade to pink. Mid-green, semi-glossy leaves on a 30cm (1ft) plant. Raised by Sean McCann, the rose journalist and amateur breeder.

Little Flirt Moore, 1961. (*R. wichuraiana* × 'Floradora') × ('Golden Glow' × 'Zee')
Pointed petals give a starlike outline to the orange-yellow flowers, which have a yellow petal reverse. A tall and very robust grower, with light

green leaves, which will reach 38cm (15in). Still a favourite after something like thirty years.

Little Len Hatfield and Buckley, 1987. Parentage not given
Two amateurs bred this one, with Hybrid Tea-shaped flowers in buff-apricot on a healthy, dark-leaved plant which reaches 30cm (1ft). Makes a very good edging rose.

Little Russell Robinson, 1983. Parentage not given
The flowers here are a warm, glowing brick-red, most unusual and striking, especially when displayed against the dark green leaves. A good show rose which makes a sturdy, 30cm (1ft) bush.

Mabel Dot Dot, 1966. 'Orient' × 'Perla de Alcanada'
Something of a curiosity and resurrected from the past by Peter Beales. One of the lesser-known roses from Pedro Dot of Spain, this one has clusters of tiny, rosy-coral, double blooms on an upright plant of 25cm (10in) with bronze-tinted, glossy foliage.

Magic Carrousel Moore, 1972. 'Little Darling' × 'Westmont'
Hardy and reliable, with large, double blooms in white with rose-red tinting on the petal edges. Very free-flowering and making a strong, branching bush to 25cm (10in) in height with healthy, dark green foliage. Good for cutting and for the show bench.

Minijet Meilland, 1977. 'Seventeen' × ('Mon Petit' × 'Perla de Montserrat')
Salmon-pink flowers of exceptional size on a short-growing, bushy plant to 23cm (9in).

Mini Metro De Ruiter, 1979. 'Minuette' × seedling
A striking vermilion-orange, the double flowers open wide to reveal golden stamens. A tall, bushy grower to 38cm (15in) with mid-green leaves. Always puts on a cheerful display.

Mona Ruth Moore, 1959. [('Soeur Therese' × 'Wilhelm') × (seedling × 'Red Ripples')] × 'Zee'
Bushy, up to 30cm (1ft) with mid-green, leathery leaves. The fully double, pink flowers are carried in clusters large and small.

Mood Music Moore, 1977. 'Fairy Moss' × 'Gold Moss'
A great step forward among the Moss rose miniatures, this one has very double, orange-pink flowers of medium size with the stems thickly encrusted with moss. Only a slight fragrance, but the plant is robust

though not particularly tall at 25cm (10in). If you want a miniature Moss rose, this is the best available at the moment.

Mr Bluebird Moore, 1960. 'Old Blush' × 'Old Blush'
This parentage is rather difficult to believe, as there is no hint of lavender-blue in any China rose, and here we have one of the oldest Chinas known to the West producing a variety in that colouring. However that may be, the flowers of 'Mr Bluebird' are only just semi-double but come with great continuity and considerable freedom on a tall, rather spindly plant that makes 25cm (10in). Close planting is advised. The lavender-blue flowers come from small, rounded buds. The leaves are a dark, matt green.

My Valentine Moore, 1975. 'Little Chief' × 'Little Curt'
Small clusters of deep red, high-centred, very double flowers give this rose considerable distinction. The dark, bronze-tinted leaves cover the 30cm (1ft) plant well.

New Penny Moore, 1962. (*R. wichuraiana* × 'Floradora') × seedling
A short, dumpy grower to about 25cm (10in) with plentiful rounded buds that open to blooms of orange-red, which rather quickly pales to coral-pink. They are double and have a slight scent. Leathery, glossy, quite healthy foliage. A long-time favourite that seems to be having something of a revival, especially with those who favour the smaller miniatures.

Oor Wullie Anderson, 1886. Parentage not given
With such a name this rose could only have come from a Scottish firm, in this case the respected Anderson Nursery of Aberdeen. Bushy and well branched, reaching about 30cm (1ft) in height, it makes a fine edging rose with shapely, very double, soft pink blooms, offset by shiny, dark green leaves.

Orange Honey Moore, 1979. 'Rumba' × 'Over the Rainbow'
Double flowers with a classic high centre at first and then opening cupped and showing their orange stamens. The flower colour is rather more yellow than orange, showing up well in contrast to the plentiful healthy, matt green leaves. A wide-spreading, bushy grower, to 25cm (10in) tall.

Orange Sunblaze (Orange Meillandina) Meilland, 1982. 'Parador' × ('Baby Bettina' × 'Duchess of Windsor')
A dense, bushy grower carrying massed, double, cupped blooms in a startling orange red. The individual clusters are not large but they come close together so that the overall effect is most striking. Light green, matt foliage. 25cm (10in). There is a climbing sport.

Over the Rainbow Moore, 1972. 'Little Darling' × 'Westmont'
This rose has been described as like a miniature 'Piccadilly' with its red
and yellow bicolor blooms. They are small, high-centred, doubled and
slightly fragrant. Vigorous and bushy and reaching 30cm (12in), with
healthy, leathery leaves.

Paint Pot Robinson, 1984. Parentage not given
This one will keep to 25cm (10in) or less, a real baby, with blooms to
match in a delicate orange-pink. They are fragrant and show up well
against the mid-green foliage.

Pallas Harkness, 1989. Parentage not given
The blooms this time are peachy-pink, intensifying towards the heart
of the flower and with a paler colour on the petal reverse.

Pandora Harkness, 1989. Parentage not given
Would fit equally well among the patio roses and one of a set of four
introduced by this hybridist in 1989. All are ideal for pots and troughs on
patios or for edging borders. The others are 'Pallas', 'Phoebe' and
'Phoenix' which see. All have a similar style; compact growth, 38cm
(15in) in height, and double flowers covering a wide range of colours. In
'Pandora' the blooms are deep cream and packed with many petals to
form ehchanting rosettes. They make good cut flowers for a small
arrangement.

Party Girl Saville, 1979. 'Rise 'n' Shine' × 'Sheri Anne'
Long, pointed buds open to 3cm (1in) flowers, double, high-centred and
fragrant. The colour is a soft yellow, and they are borne on a compact,
bushy plant that makes 25cm (10in). A rose that is only now beginning to
feature on the show bench in the United Kingdom and for which a bright
future is predicted.

Peace Sunblaze (Lady Meilander, Lady Sunblaze) Meilland, 1985.
Parentage not given
Another of the 'Sunblaze' roses with many other names, resulting
in considerable confusion for both sellers and buyers. In this case
the inclusion of the word Sunblaze seems singularly inappropriate as the
colouring is blush-pink which will, after a time, fade to white. The
flowers are double and the bushy plant will reach 38cm (15in). Despite
my strictures about the name, still a good rose.

Peachy White Moore, 1976. 'Little Darling' × 'Red Germain'
Long pointed buds open to semi-double, fragrant flowers of creamy-
white with a pink tinge. A very free bloomer, making an upright plant to
30cm (1ft), with leathery, dark green leaves.

Peon (Tom Thumb) de Vink, 1936. *R.* 'Rouletii' × 'Gloria Mundi'
At present this does not seem to be obtainable in the United Kingdom, which is certainly not as it should be as this was one of the miniatures that really put them back on the map after their early eclipse. And it is a good little rose, too. As already recounted, when it was first introduced it was a sensation, particularly on the American side of the Atlantic, not least because of its very dwarf stature. It will not top 23cm (9in) and has deep red, semi-double flowers with white centres. The leaves are light green and leathery. 'Peon' appears in the pedigree of many another miniature and must not be allowed to slip into oblivion.

Perla de Alcanada (Baby Crimson, Pearl of Canada, Titantia, Wheat-croft's Baby Crimson) Dot, 1944. 'Perle des Rouges' × *R.* 'Rouletii'
Another classic rose from the early days of the miniatures, though not so old as 'Peon'. Also a parent of many other good roses and can still stand comparison with modern varieties. The semi-double, carmine-pink flowers are produced in small clusters and sometimes singly. At 23–25cm (9–10in), it is a short, twiggy grower of compact habit with dark, glossy leaves. Will probably need yearly thinning out of the very dense growth.

Perla de Montserrat Dot, 1945. 'Cécile Brunner' × *R.* 'Rouletii'
Another cross from this Spanish breeder that has lasted very well, still selling in considerable quantities because of its enduring charm. It is a compact grower reaching only about 23cm (9in), with dark green, matt foliage which covers the plant well. The shapely blooms are carried in sprays well above the leaves and are of a soft pink, deepening towards the centres.

Petite Folie Meilland, 1968. ('Danny Robin' × 'Fire King') × ('Cri Cri' × 'Perla de Montserrat')
Bright, coral-orange flowers growing with considerable freedom on a strong-growing plant that will reach 25cm (10in).

Petit Four Ilsink, 1982. 'Marlena' seedling × seedling
A thorny, wide-spreading bush which will reach 38cm (15in), with mid-green, glossy leaves. The flowers, carried in clusters, are a good, strong pink and semi-double.

Phoebe Harkness, 1989. Parentage not given
This and the next rose form the second pair in the group of four new introductions first mentioned under the variety 'Pandora'. Small, rose-pink blooms distinguish this one.

Phoenix Harkness, 1989. Parentage not given
Here the flowers are ruby-red and have perhaps fewer petals than those of the other three, though they are still double.

Pixie Rose Dot, 1961. 'Perla de Montserrat' × 'Coralin'
A short branching variety that will make a compact bush about 23cm (9in) high with dark green, semi-glossy leaves. The deep pink flowers are high-centred at first and then open cupped. They come in both large and small clusters.

Pour Toi (For You, Para Ti, Wendy) Dot, 1946. 'Edouardo Toda' × 'Pompon de Paris'
It is strange that 'Pompon de Paris' figures in the breeding lines of so few miniatures, for here it has been the parent of one of the most successful of all time. The creamy-white flowers of 'Pour Toi' have yellowish centres and are produced in good-sized clusters on a bushy, 23cm (9in) plant. The glossy leaves tend to be rather large for the size of the bush, but this is only a minor fault.

Red Ace (Amruda, Amanda) De Ruiter, 1977. Parentage not known
A frequent winner on the show bench and equally good for garden display. Its shapely, double, deep red flowers are carried in small clusters and come with exceptional freedom and a quick repeat. Growth is bushy and compact to about 30cm (1ft) and the leaves are mid-green and semi-glossy.

Rise 'n' Shine (Golden Sunblaze, Golden Meillandina) Moore, 1978. 'Little Darling' × 'Yellow Magic'
Quite a large plant as it will reach 45cm (18in), and it bushes out reasonably well. The bright, double, yellow flowers are shapely at first but open rather formlessly, though this does not detract from the colourful show they put on if grown in the mass. Plentiful mid-green foliage which may need watching for black spot. Quite a success on the show bench.

Rosina (Josephine Wheatcroft, Yellow Sweetheart) Dot, 1951. 'Edouardo Toda' × R. 'Rouletii'
One of the short growers typical of this raiser's miniatures, as it will only reach 23cm (9in). However, it makes an upright plant covered in small clusters of semi-double, clear yellow flowers which are very quick to repeat. Watch out for black spot.

Rouletii (R. 'Rouletii') Correvon, 1922. Parentage not known
The one that started it all and from which pretty well all modern

miniatures are descended. The double, rose-pink flowers are carried singly or in small clusters on a bushy, compact plant with matt, dark green leaves. It is unlikely to top 23cm (9in) and, while there are probably better varieties nowadays for garden display, this must come at the top of the list for garden interest.

Royal Baby Bracegirdle, 1982. 'Genrosa' × 'Baby Darling'
Bright scarlet, double flowers, the petals shading to yellow towards the centre. They are carried in medium-sized trusses on a 30cm (12in) plant.

Royal Salute (Rose Baby) McGredy, 1976. 'New Penny' × 'Marlena'
Large, moderately full, rose-red blooms carried in small clusters with considerable freedom. Slightly fragrant. The leaves are dark green and semi-glossy and are carried by a plant which will reach 30cm (1ft).

Rugul (Guletta) De Ruiter, 1973. Parentage not given
A rose that deserves to be far better known than it is as it is one of the very best miniatures, constantly in flower and very healthy. The bright yellow, semi-double flowers are carried with great freedom on a bushy plant about 38cm (15in) high. Small, rich green leaves.

Sarah Robinson Robinson, 1984. Parentage not given
A beautiful apricot found in no other miniature distinguishes this lovely little rose. Shapely buds open to reveal fragrant, double flowers borne with great freedom on a plant with dark green leaves. About 30cm (1ft) is the average height.

Scarlet Gem (Scarlet Pimpernel) Meilland, 1961. ('Moulin Rouge' × 'Fashion') × ('Perla de Montserrat' × 'Perla de Alcanada')
Double, cupped flowers in a rather variable bright red. Of very upright habit to 38cm (15in), which means close planting. The dark green leaves may need protection from black spot.

Scarletta De Ruiter, 1972. Parentage not given
A tall miniature, reaching 45cm (18in) or a little more, so that it could be a patio rose if the toss of a coin decided it that way. Whichever it is, it is a very good variety with bright scarlet blooms shown off well by the glossy, mid-green leaves. Good for cutting with its long stems and it lasts well in water.

Shell Beach Robinson, 1984. Parentage not given
The pink buds open into very double, pure white blooms of great refinement. Light green foliage on a plant of average height, i.e. 25cm (10in).

Sheri Anne Moore, 1973. 'Little Darling' × 'New Penny'
Large, full, orange-red blooms with a yellow base to the petals are carried on a tall, upright plant with glossy leaves. They have a good scent and are excellent for cutting and showing. 38cm (15in).

Silver Tips Moore, 1961. (*R. wichuraiana* × 'Floradora') × 'Lilac Time'
A wide-spreading, rather sprawling bush to only 23cm (9in), of open growth with mid-green, leathery leaves. Double pink flowers with silvery-pink tips to each petal and a silvery-pink reverse.

Snowball (Angelita) McGredy, 1982. 'Moana' × 'Snow Carpet'
Growing no more than 20cm (8in) tall, this forms a dense, snowball-like mound of tiny rosette blooms in pure white. Foliage light green. Excellent for a rockery.

Snow Carpet McGredy, 1980. 'New Penny' × 'Temple Bells'
This was the first true ground-cover miniature rose and is still the only one that is dense enough to smother weeds, even if only over a comparatively small area. It may reach up to 25cm (10in) in height, but will spread out for up to 60cm (2ft) in all directions, carpeting the ground with tiny, close-packed leaflets and small, white, double flowers, most of which come at midsummer. The repeat is fitful.

Snowdrop (Amouretta, Amorette) De Ruiter, 1979. 'Rosy Jewel' × 'Zorina'
Upright to 30cm (1ft), this bushy plant carries most of its ivory-white flowers singly, but they come with such freedom that the absence of clusters is scarcely noticed. Mid-green, glossy foliage.

Stacey Sue Moore, 1976. 'Ellen Poulsen' × 'Fairy Princess'
One of the best miniatures with very double, globular flowers in light pink. They make good cut flowers and have a pleasing light fragrance. A bushy if rather lax grower, which will nevertheless reach all of 30cm (1ft).

Starina Meilland, 1965. ('Dany Robin' × 'Fire King') × 'Perla de Montserrat'
Though raised a good many years ago this still takes some beating in any collection of miniatures. The blooms are very large—some people might say too large for the plant—and extremely showy, being very full and a bright orange-red. The bush is freely branching and covered with mid-green, glossy leaves. Average height is 30cm (1ft). Makes a good cut flower and exhibition variety.

Stars 'n' Stripes Moore, 1976. 'Little Chief' × ('Little Darling' × 'Ferdinand Pichard')
It was the latter rose, a Hybrid Perpetual, that passed on the pink and white striping of its petals to produce something that was unique among miniatures when 'Stars 'n' Stripes' was first introduced. There, however, the resemblance ended, for though the miniature's flowers are quite shapely at first, they open rather formlessly and could do with rather more petals. In the mass, however, they make a striking and unusual display. Rather lax in growth, but vigorous enough, and making 25cm (10in) in height.

Suma Onodera, 1989. bred from 'Nozomi'
A vast improvement on the earlier rose and not only because it has a much longer flowering season. It grows in much the same way, no more than 25cm (10in) high, but spreading out up to 1m (3ft) all round, hugging the ground and so ideal for underplanting or for tumbling over a low wall. The flowers come in clusters all along the branches, double and ruby-red, opening to reveal golden stamens. It has none of the rather washed-out look 'Nozomi' can sometimes take on after a while.

Sweet Fairy de Vink, 1946. 'Peon' × seedling
One of the smallest of the lot, reaching no more than 15cm (6in) in height but making a perfectly proportioned bush with tiny, dark green, glossy leaves. The double flowers are a soft, blush-pink and open cupped. If you can get down to smell them you will discover that they are fragrant.

Teeny Weeny Poulsen, 1986. Parentage not given
Deep rose-pink blooms borne in good-sized trusses and very free-flowering. A low, compact bush with mid-green, glossy leaves. Probably 23cm (10in) in height.

Tom Thumb (see 'Peon').

Toy Clown Moore, 1966. 'Little Darling' × 'Magic Wand'
Medium-sized blooms, white edged carmine, slightly cupped in shape, which are carried in good-sized clusters on a bushy plant which will reach 30cm (1ft). Many people now consider that 'Magic Carrousel' is a better rose of similar colouring, but 'Toy Clown' remains on many nursery lists and clearly has its adherents.

Wee Man (Tapis de Soie) McGredy, 1974. 'Little Flirt' × 'Marlena'
Clusters of large, semi-double flowers in rich scarlet. The dark green, glossy foliage will need watching for black spot. Despite this, 'Wee Man' has been a successful parent of a number of patio roses, in particular those from the Cocker nursery of Aberdeen. Will probably reach 25cm (10in).

Woodland Lady Robinson, 1984. Parentage not given
Semi-double, orange-pink blooms light up this tiny rose, contrasting well
with the dark green, glossy leaves. Up to 30cm (1ft).

Yellow Doll Moore, 1962. 'Golden Glow' × 'Zee'
Very large, full blooms on a tall grower that may well reach 38cm (15in)
but bushes out well. It may need disease protection but is a worthwhile
rose if well cared for, for its pleasing light yellow colouring.

Yellow Sunblaze (Yellow Meillandina) Meilland, 1980. [Poppy Flash' ×
('Charleston' × 'Allgold')] × 'Gold Coin'
This makes a sturdy, 38cm (15in) plant with double, yellow flowers,
edged pink, freely carried in large trusses. A slight scent.

Yorkshire Sunblaze (White Meillandina) Meilland, 1983. 'Katherina
Zeimet' × 'White Gem'
Small clusters of semi-double, white flowers on a bushy grower that will
reach 25cm (10in). Plentiful light green foliage.

CHAPTER 5

CLIMBING ROSES

The history of the climbing rose is much less clear cut than that of most other kinds of rose and no obvious single line of development emerges. There have been, rather, a number of individual climbing or semi-climbing roses which were discovered in the wild and which were used to found what were usually quite small dynasties. A number of these, like the Noisettes, were gradually absorbed into the main stream and lost their identity quite early on. In their case it was the sprawling Musk rose rather than a climber that provided the climbing element, while with other roses it was ramblers which were involved. The European species, *R. semper-virens* for instance, white-flowered and rather tender so that it is seldom seen in the United Kingdom, produced such distinguished climbing offspring as 'Félicité Perpétue' and 'Adélaïde d'Orléans'. Or again, another European rose *R. arvenis* (The Field Rose) that could just be described as a climber, though it is really a scrambler through other shrubs, was the founder of the Ayrshire rose family, a few of which such as 'Dundee Rambler' and 'Ayrshire Splendens' can still be found in the catalogues of specialist growers. *R. arvensis* itself, a native of the British Isles, has white flowers like those of *R. sempervirens*, and is not quite such a rarity. At one time, judging by past accounts, it was common in the hedgerows, especially in shady places, and may well be the origin of the Musk rose that Shakespeare so often mentions.

Most ramblers and climbers, however, came from much further afield and were only really to become garden plants in Victorian times. Early in the nineteenth century, *R. polyantha* arrived from the East. As recounted in the chapter on patio roses, it was later to have its name changed to *R. multiflora* and to become the founder of the group known as Multiflora ramblers, which included the multicoloured 'Seven Sisters' rose, 'Hiawatha' from America, 'Violette' and 'Veilchenblau'.

However, the influence of all these was as nothing compared to a Chinese species called *R. wichuraiana*, which was a parent of many fine ramblers but also, through 'New Dawn' and others, of numerous climbers. *R. gigantea* from China has also played some part, though not a

71

very extensive one, in the development of climbing roses, but it is surprising how few of the many wild roses have been made use of. Instead, climbing sports have been extensively grown, much more so in past times than now. These, however, provided really nothing very new for they were simply roses already known in their bush form.

For the first half of this century, up to the 1950s and early 1960s, year after year the nursery catalogues contained virtually the same varieties: 'Mme Grégoire Staechelin', 'Climbing Mrs Herbert Stevens', 'Climbing Etoile de Hollande', 'Paul's Lemon Pillar', 'Mme Alfred Carrière', 'Mrs Sam McGredy' and so on, plus the ramblers 'Dorothy Perkins', 'Albertine' and 'Albéric Barbier'. One could see the reason for this from the growers' point of view, for most gardeners do not buy more than one or two climbers where they might buy a dozen or more bush roses. Breeding a new rose takes a long time and much patient work, so it seemed to make sense for the hybridists to concentrate on what would bring them the best return financially. They were, after all, in the rose business to earn a living.

It was not until a few brave and more far-seeing spirits like Sam McGredy (then still in Ireland) and Wilhelm Kordes in Germany began to experiment and came up with varieties such as 'Casino' and 'School-girl', and 'Dortmund' and 'Hamburger Phoenix', that anything much new appeared. Other breeders began to join them and once people saw the new climbers they liked them and began to buy.

When discussing climbing roses for the small garden, size is not quite so vital a matter as it is with other kinds of rose. However limited your space may be laterally, it is not likely to be seriously curtailed vertically. The sky, or at least the height of your house, is the limit. Just the same there will be small gardens where low walls are the only possible places for siting climbing roses. There may also be other such limitations which make the less vigorous climbers essential, and it will really be the nature of the supports available—and all climbing roses need some form of support—that will determine which roses you can grow.

At the other end of the scale a house may have walls 9m (30ft) high on which a rose can run riot, even if the rest of the garden is little more than a back yard and the rose the only plant in it. However, in the selection of varieties that follows I have tended towards choosing roses that do not get too vast and which cover their supports well low down as well as high up with both foliage and flowers. There are no tree-climbers in the selection, but there are some rare roses. Part of the aim of this book, as will I hope be clear by now, is to produce rose gardens which are different, and a few really unusual varieties help towards this provided, of course, that they are good roses as well as being less often seen. All of them are available from specialist growers.

The question of remontancy in roses for a small garden has already been discussed; whether or not a rose keeps flowering right through into the autumn or just puts on one spectacular display at midsummer. A climber takes up a lot of space. It may cover a whole wall or fence and so should really work for its living. Most of the roses I have chosen are fairly continuous in their flowering, or at least have two great flushes of bloom per season. There are few ramblers among them, but those that are included are outstanding, even though they do not bloom in the autumn. Their one display is breathtaking, but before taking my word for this and committing yourself to a once-flowering rose, try to see it growing somewhere. There are many of the gardens of The National Trust—among others—that still have fine displays of rambling roses. And with luck they will be labelled.

It has been said that roses are not true climbing plants because they do not have tendrils to twine around their supports or suckers to grasp them by. Botanically I suppose that this is true, but a plant that can scale a tree to the height of 12m (40ft) or more, as some climbing roses can, or which can cover the wall of a substantial house, is to me a climbing plant. A rose uses its prickles (they are not, strictly speaking, thorns) to hook over the branches and twigs of a tree through which it wishes to climb; just as efficient a climbing aid as tendrils or suckers. However, I suppose it could be argued (and doubtless will be) that a rose does, in the garden at any rate, need something else to keep it in place. With the far from natural supports with which we provide it, it does need to be tied in with something and be directed where to go. There is a chemical inhibitor in each climbing rose which will stop the buds on the flowering shoots low down from breaking into growth. If the rose is allowed to grow more or less straight upwards, as it will do if left to its own devices, it will flower just at the top and be viewable only from the bedroom windows. Bend the shoots over towards the horizontal, however, and the inhibitor ceases to function. Flowers will appear all along the shoots and for this reason climbing roses should always be fanned out sideways, not only to cover as much of a wall as possible, but to ensure that there is the maximum possible bloom at all levels.

What can one do if one has a house with walls broken up by windows, often quite close together, so that it is not possible to spread out the canes of a climbing rose very far? Well, for these situations there are a number of roses, some not very vigorous climbers and some extra-vigorous shrubs, which will fill the bill admirably and not just flower at the ends of the shoots. The selection in this chapter contains a number of them.

And what about roses for pillars? Pillars on their own, that is, or else the pillars that support a pergola and up which a rose will have to climb before it can be trained along the top. Pillars go straight up and down, so the answer is to spiral the rose shoots around the uprights and this will give very much the same effect as training them horizontally on wires on

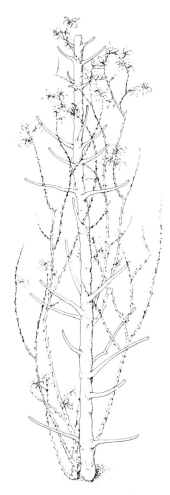

10 Training a climbing rose on a larch pillar, with sections
of the branches left to which roses can be tied

a wall. The flowers will appear low down as well as at the top.

On a wall or fence the shoots can be fixed with plastic ties to horizontal wires threaded through vine eyes driven into the wood or brickwork. These will hold the shoots about 8–10cm (3–4in) from the wall surface to allow for air circulation which will help to minimise disease. If there is difficulty in driving the vine eyes into the bricks or the mortar between them, holes can first be made with a 0.5mm (³⁄₁₆in) drill and the vine eyes, which are tapered, driven firmly into the holes.

Although our priority in a small garden must be for remontant roses, it cannot be denied that once-flowering ramblers are the best for covering arches, pergolas and the like, where the extra flexibility of their canes

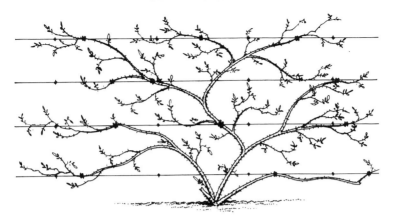

11 Training a climber on a wall

gives them great advantages when it comes to training. However, recurrent climbers can certainly be used, provided that the training of those with the stiffest shoots starts early while they are still reasonably pliable and can be directed without too much of a struggle wherever you wish them to go.

A climbing rose does, like any other rose, like to be in full sun, but achieving this in a small garden may sometimes be a problem. The only wall available may well be the wall of your house and face north, so does that mean that a climbing rose is out of the question? Not really. Nursery catalogues often list roses as being suitable for north walls and these might include, from the selection of roses in this chapter, varieties like 'Dortmund', 'Leverkusen', 'Maigold', 'New Dawn' and, best of all, 'Morning Jewel'. However, it must be said that no rose, however amenable, will do other than tolerate a north wall, some better than others. All will perform much better in the sun, provided that they can have sunshine for at the very least half the day. It is not simply a question of hot sun to bring the flowers out, but of ripening the wood of the shoots so that they can withstand the winter frosts.

It is often asked if roses can be grown in a small town garden consisting only of a paved area. The answer is an emphatic yes, in two ways. Either a paving stone can be lifted and, provided that there is reasonable soil under it, the rose can be planted in that—suitably enriched with bonemeal and if possible with compost—or else climbers can be grown very successfully in containers. These must be of sufficient size, and watering is of first importance. A half-barrel would be of ideal size for a climbing rose, but more details of planting roses in containers will be found in Chapter 7.

A point to bear in mind when choosing a climber for the wall of your house is the colour of your brickwork or rendering, and also of your paintwork. A pale yellow rose such as 'Leverkusen' might be wasted against a buff-coloured wall, or a white rose against white rendering, while roses in certain red shades might clash horribly with certain brick colours. Colour stability is of great importance in a climbing rose too, for if the blooms become unsightly after a while they are not easy to remove. In the same way, resistance to rain is very important and whether or not a rose sheds its petals cleanly after flowering. It was for these latter reasons that I have not included the very popular 'Danse du Feu' in our selection for small gardens because, opening the most exciting flaming scarlet, it very soon changes to an unattractive dull red. If it rains the old blooms quickly turn brown and hang on the plant like sodden paper bags. Not a sight to gladden the heart.

Should you decide that you really cannot resist a particular once-flowering climber, there is an easy way of prolonging the flowering period, or at least the period when there is colour. This is either to grow it up through another wall shrub that flowers at a different time, or else to grow something else up through it, a late-flowering clematis, perhaps. These as a rule are the kinds of clematis that benefit from being cut almost to the ground each spring and this is a great advantage if they are to be grown up through a rose. A small-flowered species clematis will very soon create an impenetrable tangle which could suffocate the rose.

It is not, of course, necessary to concentrate entirely on wall plants that flower when the roses are over. They can be very effective with remontant roses too, and it does not take much imagination to see how beautiful the combination of a white rose like 'Climbing Iceberg' and a blue ceanothus can be. Climbing roses, whether in combination with other plants or not, can make the ugliest building look beautiful. Harriet Beecher Stowe, the author of *Uncle Tom's Cabin*, knew what they could do and wrote: 'The whole front of it was covered with a large scarlet begonia and a native multiflora rose, which entwisting and interlacing left scarce a vestige of rough logs to be seen.' An image hardly to be spoiled by the knowledge that *R. multiflora* is not a native of the USA.

Even the smallest of gardens can be divided into more than one part, and what better to lead from one to the other than a tunnel of roses? Admittedly the very smallest garden would hardly accommodate a pergola, but it could probably just manage an arch. Space is going to govern the size of any structure and in fact a pergola need not take up so much room if one side is made up from a boundary fence. However, free-standing or not, the most economical type of pergola or arch can be made from rustic poles by anyone handy with a hammer and saw. It will not, however, last for more than about three years unless it is properly weatherproofed—the whole arch and not just the points where the uprights enter the soil.

Metal arches and pergolas can be bought and, though not so attractive to look at at first, will soon be hidden beneath the foliage. They should

12 Training a climbing rose on a pergola or an arch

last a long time, especially those that are covered in a thick plastic coating which keeps rust at bay, but brick pillars for a pergola would be the most permanent of all. However, with their footings, they need considerably more skill to construct and take up much more room, coupled with which they are not nearly so easy to train a rose up as there are no cross-bracings to tie the rose in to.

If you are making an arch, whatever material you choose to use do not forget that you may wish to push a fully loaded wheelbarrow through it and it is amazing how wide such a thing can be. Less than 1.5m (5ft) of width and you may be in difficulties.

Varieties of climbing rose

Alchymist ('Alchemist' in many catalogues) Kordes, 1956. 'Golden Glow' × *R. rubiganosa* hybrid
Not the best rose to start my list with as it is one of the non-remontant ones, but it is such a good rose and so little known that no opportunity should be lost in bringing it before a wider public. The blooms, unfortunately carried only at midsummer, are a bright golden-buff, with their many petals opening flat like an old garden rose to reveal a golden-

77

orange centre. Very striking and perhaps one could compare it to a greatly refined 'Gloire de Dijon'. Excellent bronze-green foliage and a vigour that will take it to about 3.7m (12ft).

Alister Stella Gray (Golden Rambler) George Paul, 1894. Parentage not known
Despite its American name (shown in brackets), this is not a once-flowering variety as most ramblers are, but one of the best repeat flowerers there is. Many climbers are described in nursery catalogues as being 'always in flower', but few avoid a pretty long late summer gap between their two main flushes of bloom. These, with 'Alister Stella Gray', may not be particularly spectacular, but it is seldom without flowers from mid-June till late October, the autumn blooming being perhaps more prolific than the earlier one. The tightly scrolled buds open to a bright buff-yellow which quickly pales as the flowers unfurl. They are double, about 5cm (2in) across, and have the petals neatly quartered. Medium-sized trusses are usual early on with much larger ones later in the season. It is not a dense grower and has slender, almost thornless shoots in the early stages of growth. Later they become more fiercely armed. The protection of a warm wall will be of benefit, on which this rose should reach about 3.7m (12ft).

Allen Chandler Chandler, 1923. 'Hugh Dickson' × unnamed variety
Though of considerable age, this rose has yet to be bettered in its particular colour range. The semi-double flowers are a brilliant scarlet, larger than those of most climbers, and are carried with fine continuity throughout the summer and well into the autumn. They come on long stems, which makes them good for cutting, though as this rose will go up to 4.5m (15ft) they will not always be easy to reach. This also applies when it comes to dead-heading, which will markedly improve the autumn display but, if it proves impossible to carry this out, it will be found that orange-red hips will take the place of some of the late blooms. An RNRS Gold Medal was awarded in 1923.

Aloha Boerner, 1949. 'Mercedes Gallart' × 'New Dawn'
This fine American rose has taken a long time to win recognition. Nowadays it is constantly being recommended and appearing in more and more nursery lists as the result of a sustained campaign by its devotees, in which I like to think I have played no small part. It will make a good small shrub and as such could well have appeared in an earlier section of this book. With regular, fairly heavy pruning it stays at about 1.2m (4ft) when planted in the open. Against a wall, however, it will, over four or five years, climb slowly to about 2.4–3m (8–10ft), with strong

canes carrying the finest of glossy leaves that seldom if ever are attacked by either black spot or mildew.

The flower buds look unpromising in their early stages and could not be called shapely, but they soon open into the most beautiful flowers, 10–13cm (4–5in) across, very double in the old rose fashion, sweetly scented, just about rainproof despite the number of petals, and carried in small clusters on long, strong, almost thornless shoots which make them ideal for cutting. The very length of the flower stems is, however, something of a disadvantage in a climber, especially in wet weather, in that the weight of water in the blooms makes them hang out, away from the wall surface. But this is the only minus—and not a very important one—that can be chalked up against an otherwise great rose. The colour is a fine strong pink, with an orange flush in the centre of the blooms early on.

Altissimo Delbard-Chabert, 1966. 'Tenor' × unknown seedling
A short climber to 2.1–2.4m (7–8ft) with large, seven-petalled, deep crimson blooms carried in small clusters and sometimes singly. Healthy, dark green foliage covers the plant well. Remontant and a good choice for growing in a wall space between two windows where it is difficult, if not impossible, to fan out the shoots sideways.

Amadis (Crimson Boursault) Laffay, 1829. Parentage uncertain
One of the small family of Boursault roses, which are all nearly thornless and moderately vigorous climbers. It sends up long, strong shoots which turn from green to purplish-brown with age and which carry the double, cupped, deep crimson-purple flowers in large and small clusters. They come very early in the season with usually (but not, it must be said, invariably) some more to come later. It will be out at the same time as the early yellow species roses such as *R. hugonis* and *R. primula* and consorts particularly well with them. Makes a good pillar rose, reaching some 2.5m (8ft) in height, and is a joy to train because of the absence of prickles.

Blush Noisette Noisette, 1817. Seedling of 'Champney's Pink Cluster'
This will make a fine, lax shrub, but as a climber it will go up to about 3.7m (12ft) on a wall, its almost thornless shoots well covered with mid-green leaves and carrying from midsummer onwards, in clusters of varying size, small, double, cupped, deep pink flowers. These open to show golden stamens and eventually fade to a pale lilac-pink. A sweet scent is an added attraction. The crown popularly accorded to 'Zéphirine Drouhin' as the only thornless climber is, it will be noted, already beginning to slip.

Céline Forestier Trouillard, 1842. Probably a Noisette and showing the Tea Rose influence

Sometimes difficult to establish and benefiting from the protection of a wall, on which it will reach 2.4–3m (8–10ft) in time. Light green leaves and flowers borne singly or in small clusters, a creamy-yellow and with a powerful Tea Rose scent. They are very double and on opening reflex into a flat, quartered bloom. There will be a good show in the autumn as well as early on.

Compassion (Belle de Londres) Harkness, 1973. 'White Cockade' × 'Prima Ballerina'
Certainly the best climber raised in recent times, vigorous, healthy, and with fine, dark green, glossy leaves and small clusters of sizeable, beautifully shaped, apricot-pink blooms which have a fragrance that won them the Edland Medal in the RNRS trials. They appear in two main flushes, early in the summer and again in the autumn, but there will also be plenty of flowers in between. An especially good quality of this rose is the freedom with which it puts up new growth from the base, so that, if grown against a wall, it will cover it low down without having to be constantly cut back to encourage new shoots. Perhaps 4.5m (15ft) will be reached in such a situation and rather less on a pillar. Wall protection always encourages a rose to make more growth than it would in the open.

Crimson Descant Cant, 1972. 'Dortmund' × 'Etenard'
'Etenard' has 'New Dawn' blood in it, which is an advantage for any rose, and many of the latter's good qualities have been passed on to this offspring. Its crimson flowers are large, double (30 petals) and freely borne on a plant that will reach 3m (10ft) on a wall. They are fragrant and remontant and the health of this rose is above average.

Debutante Walsh, 1902. *R. wichuraiana* × 'Baroness Rothschild'
A once-flowering rambler with some similarity to 'Dorothy Perkins' and with all of that rose's good qualities and none of its bad ones. That means there is no mildew and the flowers are, perhaps, a little softer in their colouring. It carries long sprays of its cupped, rose-pink blooms, which tend to fade a little after a while. The leaves are typical of *R. wichuraiana* hybrids, neat, rounded, glossy and plentiful, and all told this is just about the best of the pink ramblers, if a little difficult to get hold of. An excellent rose with which to carry out some of the suggestions made at the beginning of this chapter: try it in partnership with a white clematis. It makes about 3m (10ft) in height.

Dortmund Kordes, 1955. Seedling × *R. kordesii*
Provided that some dead-heading is done, this is a fully remontant climber of moderate vigour—about 2.4–2.7m (8–9ft) tall—which will make a fine pillar rose and will also do admirably on a wall or fence. The

flowers are large and single, crimson with a white eye, and extremely striking. They have attractively waved petals and are carried on a plant with good, glossy foliage. It can be grown successfully as a lax, free-standing shrub, but even as a climber its height is not such as to make the recommended dead-heading an impossibility.

Dreaming Spires Mattock, 1973. 'Buccaneer' × 'Arthur Bell'
The worth of this golden-yellow climber is only slowly being recognised, which is surprising because, apart from 'Golden Showers', there is very little else to choose from in bright yellow. The blooms are large and moderately full and carried on a strong-growing plant which will reach about 2.4m (8ft), branching out well. The clustered blooms have a good scent, which is one up on 'Golden Showers' but, despite this, it has been the latter which has captured and held the public's attention. Once this has happened it is very difficult to change things, but 'Dreaming Spires' is nothing if not persistent. It is a good repeat-flowerer, too.

Dublin Bay McGredy, 1976. 'Bantry Bay' × 'Altissimo'
Many a curse has been heaped on the head of this rose as it has sat contentedly in countless rosebeds and refused point blank to climb. However, this does not always happen and, even when it does, a certain amount of patience may be rewarded when it gradually starts to gain a bit of altitude. Not more than about 2.4m (8ft), though, when nothing can be lovelier than seeing a pillar clothed in its shiny, green leaves and glowing with its large and moderately full, bright crimson blooms. Only a slight scent, but it makes a nice rose, even if it stays as a large bush.

Galway Bay McGredy, 1966. 'Heidelberg' × 'Queen Elizabeth'
Any rose with 'Queen Elizabeth''s genes pushing at it from below would be hard put to keep at ground level, but just the same 'Galway Bay' is not an especially tall climber, only reaching 2.7m (9ft) or so. The double flowers are salmon-pink and cupped in shape when fully open. They are carried in small trusses with astonishing freedom and have a good repeat. A highly recommended rose for a wall, fence, pillar or archway in a garden of whatever size.

Gerbe Rose Fauque, 1904. *R. wichuraiana* × 'Baroness Rothschild'
The same parentage, be it noted, as 'Debutante' but this time, so unpredictable are the ways of rose breeding, the outcome is at least partially remontant. The almost thornless, red shoots carry leaves much larger than is usual with a Wichuraiana hybrid, but they retain the rose's gloss. The flowers are a soft, creamy-pink, loosely double and sometimes quartered. A fine fragrance completes the picture of a notable rose and a very unusual one, not widely stocked. Buy it for a pillar as it will not go over 2.4m (8ft) or so.

Golden Showers Lammerts, 1957. 'Charlotte Armstrong' × 'Captain Thomas'
One of the best and most popular of modern climbers of moderate vigour, up to 2.4m (8ft) or so, but carrying its flowers at all levels. They come with great freedom on long, almost thornless stems, opening from slender buds to large, bright yellow, loosely formed, double blooms, which quickly fade to a much paler colour. Both shades of yellow are thus carried on the plants at the same time, making a not unattractive combination. Healthy, dark green leaves which could, perhaps, be rather more plentiful. A good rose for a pillar or, like 'Altissimo', for filling the space between two tall windows. It will also make a good, free-standing shrub.

It may be wondered whether, with their long stems, the flowers will hang out away from a wall after rain, as described as happening with 'Aloha', but with 'Golden Showers' this is not the case. The blooms have too few petals to gather much weight of water, unlike the very double, sumptuous flowers of 'Aloha'. They stay close to home and the long stems make them excellent for cutting. They last well in water.

Goldfinch Paul, 1907
A Multiflora hybrid, probably from the rose 'Hélène', which has 'Crimson Rambler' in its parentage.

Very vigorous and freely branching, though not achieving any very great height, reaching only 2.4m (8ft). It can, in fact, make a sprawling bush, almost thornless and with fine, bright green, glossy leaves. The flowers are strongly scented, small, semi-double and carried in clusters. They open a deep golden-yellow but soon fade, leaving the dark yellow stamens very prominent. There is no second blooming. When cut for the house, if this is done while the rose is in bud, the full colour will be retained.

Grand Hotel McGredy, 1972. 'Brilliant' × 'Heidelberg'
One of the least known of the McGredy climbers of the '70s and, like some of the others, half a shrub and half a climber. If trained to grow in the latter role it will not go much over 2.4m (8ft), but there are many uses for a rose of this size in a small garden and 'Grand Hotel' is every bit as good as many which are more widely known. The scarlet blooms are large, moderately full, and repeat well in the autumn. The scent is only slight, but there are fine, glossy leaves.

Guinée Mallerin, 1938. 'Souvenir de Claudius Denoyel' × 'Ami Quinard'
The latter rose was a dark crimson Hybrid Tea and it has passed on its colouring to 'Guinée' with something more added, a velvety quality to the petals which is much prized. It can be quite a strong grower but as a

rule keeps to about 3m (10ft) in height, with mid-green, leathery foliage. The blooms are large, shapely at first but opening flat to show off their yellow stamens. A most satisfying fragrance makes this an outstanding rose, but one that needs careful placing because, against a dark background, it will be largely lost, so dark is its own colouring. Keep a lookout for mildew.

Helen Knight Knight, 1966
Possibly a hybrid between *R. ecae* and *R. pimpinellifolia altaica*, found in Wisley Garden by the then Director, Frank Knight.

As this is close to being a species or wild rose, it cannot be expected that it will be remontant, but it is something very special and should not be dismissed on that account. It is, I think, really a bush rose that can be persuaded without much difficulty to climb, and in its habit and general appearance it follows quite closely many of the other early-flowering yellow species such as 'Canarybird'. The single, yellow flowers, only slightly fragrant, are carried all along the very thorny shoots, which are also clothed in delicate, fern-like leaves. Against a wall it will easily go up to 2.4–3m (8–10ft) and in spring will be the most enchanting sight, its branches fanning out wide against the surface of the wall.

Highfield Harkness, 1981
A sport from 'Compassion' (which see) and in every way its counterpart in light yellow.

Iceberg Cant, 1968. Climbing sport of the bush variety and a good one
Climbing sports do not always behave as the bushes from which they have come, many of them being shy of flowering more than once and, in the case of some like 'Climbing Peace', being shy of flowering at all, at least in the climate of the United Kingdom. No such problems with 'Climbing Iceberg' however, though it may take several years for it to achieve a second flush of bloom as good as the first. However, there will, even in its early days, always be some flowers showing right through August, a blank month with many climbers. They, like those of the bush 'Iceberg', are carried in clusters, are white and moderately full, sometimes touched with pink. The plant will reach 3.7 (12ft) on a wall, freely branching so that most of the wall will be hidden beneath the bright green, glossy, rather pointed leaves. It might be as well to keep a watch for both mildew and black spot, but in many gardens the rose is perfectly healthy.

Joseph's Coat Armstrong and Swim, 1964. 'Buccaneer' × 'Circus'
A short climber or a wide-spreading bush, 'Joseph's Coat' is equally good in either form, making a cheerful display with its large, double, multi-

coloured flowers. They open a bright orange-yellow, changing to orange-red and then to pink, rather after the habit of the Floribunda 'Masquerade', but with none of the latter's rather dingy tones in the final stages. On a wall, the flowers keep coming at all levels if the bush is fanned out to its maximum spread of about 1.8m (6ft). Its height will be about the same, so that it is an ideal rose for a low wall or fence. It is fully remontant, though there is likely to be a gap between flushes. The leaves are dark and glossy. A rather neglected rose which deserves to be better known. It is infinitely better than 'Climbing Masquerade', the only other one in the same colour range.

Kathleen Harrop Dickson, 1919
A fragrant, soft shell-pink sport of 'Zéphirine Drouhin', which see. Perhaps rather less vigorous, making 2.4m (8ft), and to my mind a more attractive pink, though it has never caught on in the same way as the original.

Leverkusen Kordes, 1955. *R. kordesii* × 'Golden Glow'
One of the many climbers and climber/shrubs bred by this German hybridist especially to withstand the harsh north German winters, and hence a really tough rose that will thrive nearly anywhere. Rather later into flower than most, it carries a great profusion of long sprays of double, lemon-yellow flowers with a spicy fragrance. These, shapely at first, open wide to reveal yellow stamens. It would I think, be more widely planted if its continuity of flowering were better, for there is apt to be a longish gap between the first and second flushes of bloom. On a wall it will go up to 3m (10ft) or so, less on a pillar, and it will make a free-standing shrub. Some reports say that mildew can be a problem, but I have never found this myself.

Mme Ernst Calvat Schwartz, 1888
A lighter pink sport of 'Mme Isaac Pereire' but otherwise similar to it in every way. Perhaps the colour of this one is better against a red brick wall.

Mme Isaac Pereire Garçon, 1881. Parentage not known
A Bourbon shrub, so what is it doing here? The answer is simple. A number of the less vigorous climbers I have indicated will make good shrubs and here the reverse applies. A number of the more robust Bourbons, Moss roses and some others will make excellent climbers as long as you do not expect them to exceed about 2.4m (8ft) in height. This is one of them, a rose with sumptuous, double blooms in deep cerise-pink, richly fragrant and with a fine autumn performance. The very sturdy shoots, with their large, leathery leaves, will need firm tying in if they are to be properly controlled.

Maigold Kordes, 1953. 'Poulsen's Pink' × 'Frühlingstag'
A Pimpinellifolia hybrid, which shows in its fierce armoury of thorns. Apart from that, only a greater degree of remontance could improve it, for after the first dramatic flush there is only likely to be very spasmodic bloom. The flowers are large, semi-double and apricot-yellow, carried in such profusion that they will almost entirely cover the plant and hide the excellent, tough, glossy leaves. Prompt dead-heading will help to increase late flowering, and certainly a hot summer such as that of 1989 will do so. In an average year 'Maigold' should, true to its name, be in bloom before the end of May and continue to put on a brave show for up to six weeks. After that, what you get is something of a toss-up. About 4.5m (15ft) will be the usual maximum height, so it is a strong grower. You will need stout gloves when you prune or train it because of the multitude of thorns.

Morning Jewel Cocker, 1968. 'New Dawn' × 'Red Dandy'
One of the many first-rate offspring of 'New Dawn' (which see). The fairly full, cupped flowers are bright pink and will first appear at midsummer in a tremendous flush which will cover the plant at all levels, for this is a plant that breaks freely at the base and sends out plenty of lateral growth. The second flush will be rather less spectacular, but still very well worth while. On a wall about 3m (10ft) will be reached, which is enough for the majority of situations, and leaf coverage will be good when the rose is not in flower. Robust health is another point in 'Morning Jewel''s favour and, with so many good qualities, it is a pity that it is not stocked more widely. There are signs, however, that word-of-mouth recommendation is having its effect and that its worth is slowly beginning to be appreciated.

Mrs Herbert Stevens, Climbing
A climbing sport of the bush form, the parents of which were 'Frau Karl Druschki' × 'Niphetos'; raised by Pernet-Ducher in 1922.
This is a climbing Tea rose, a family generally considered too tender for growing in the United Kingdom. The climbing form of 'Mrs Herbert Stevens' is, however, perfectly hardy and will grow anywhere, even on poor light soils. It will reach perhaps 4.5m (15ft), the long elegant buds with which it is laden opening into shapely, medium-sized, creamy-white blooms with a delicious fragrance. They come singly or in small clusters with a good repeat, the only question mark hanging over them being how well they will stand up to rain, for the petals are thin and papery.

Mutabilis (Tipo Ideal)
Origin uncertain, but a China rose hybrid of considerable antiquity.
For those who have never seen this rose either in its bush or in its

climbing form it will come as a considerable eye-opener, especially for those who think that the Floribunda 'Masquerade' was the first rose to change colour dramatically (as opposed to fading) as it aged. For the loosely formed, double blooms of 'Mutabilis' open the soft buff-yellow of a chamois leather, on the second day change to a coppery-pink, and later still become a coppery-crimson. All stages will be on the plant at the same time, giving the effect of dancing butterflies, for the blooms come with great freedom, especially in the first flush in June. There will, however, always be some flowers to see, right through to the autumn, when the second flush occurs. The shoots are a dark plum-red and the foliage a coppery-green. In normal circumstances it will climb to about 3m (10ft) but in the garden of Kiftsgate Court in Gloucestershire it has reached 9m (30ft) or more on the house wall. This is, however, exceptional, and it will be quite suitable for a small garden in the normal run of things. As a matter of fact it will also make a small, spreading bush of no more than 1.2m (4ft) in height, in which form it will be equally floriferous.

New Dawn

A repeat-flowering sport of the once-flowering Wichuraiana rambler 'Dr Van Fleet' and a rose that set the pattern for generations to come when it was introduced in 1930 by Henry A. Dreer in the USA. It was discovered growing in the Somerset Nurseries of New Brunswick, New Jersey, and a very large proportion of the climbing roses introduced since then have 'New Dawn' either as a parent or grandparent.

It has passed on its many good qualities to most of them, for it is an adaptable, healthy rose that will thrive in most situations. Primarily a lateral grower, it will be most happy on a low fence or in scrambling up and along a pergola, rather than in scaling a high wall, though it will do that too, since it may reach some 4.5m (15ft). It will also climb trees with considerable enthusiasm.

The fragrant blooms are carried in medium-sized trusses and are soft pink with a slightly deeper flush in the centre. They are carried with great freedom in the first flush at midsummer and from that time onward the plant will never be without flowers. There will, however, be no repeat of that first, breathtaking display.

Paul Lede Lowe, 1913. Sport from the bush form bred by Pernet-Ducher in 1913

A climbing Tea rose of great merit but almost unknown. Vigorous to about 4.5m (15ft), it carries a good coverage of healthy, dark green leaves and strongly scented, double flowers, yellowish-buff in colour, shading to carmine at the centre. Very striking with 'The Alchymist', I suppose, the nearest comparison. However, this one is fully remontant.

Phyllis Bide Bide, 1923. 'Perle d'Or' × 'Gloire de Dijon'
'Phyllis Bide' won an RNRS Gold Medal in 1924 and then lapsed into comparative obscurity, as can happen for no discernible reason, even to a first-class rose such as this one. It is also very different from anything else and, though it is not a particularly strong grower, it is a climber more continuously in flower than any other I can think of and of inestimable value in a small garden. It will probably not top 2.4m (8ft), but will spread out well, bearing large clusters of small, semi-double blooms in a combination of pale, primrose yellow and pink. There is not usually the conventional first flush but instead there will be a steady stream of bloom for fully six months of the year.

Pink Perpetue Gregory, 1965. 'Danse du Feu' × 'New Dawn'
One of the best all-purpose climbers produced since the last war, useful for a wall, pillar, arch or fence with a good lateral spread and dense, semi-glossy leaf coverage right to the ground. The double, cupped flowers in small trusses come at all levels, too, up to a maximum height of about 2.4m (8ft), which 'Pink Perpetue' will take some time to achieve. The blooms are two-tone pink, with a deeper carmine shade on the petal reverses. The first flush can only be described as generous in the extreme and, provided that a thorough dead-heading is carried out, will be repeated in the autumn. However, even if the dead-heading is skipped there will still be a good show of late flowers.

Ramona (Red Cherokee) Dietrich and Turner, 1913. A sport from 'Anemone', a *R. laevigata* hybrid
Not a rose for a spectacular display and a rather sparse, angular grower, though it will make 2.7m (9ft). It will benefit from a warm wall as it has a reputation for not being completely hardy. The foliage is glossy and could be more plentiful, and by now the reader must be wondering what this rose has to recommend it. It is the flowers, as might have been guessed, and they are large, single, and of a glowing cerise-crimson with delicately veined petals, resembling in some ways a particularly beautiful large-flowered clematis. Very special but do not count on many late blooms.

Rosy Mantle Cocker, 1968. 'New Dawn' × 'Prima Ballerina'
This rose has inherited the colour, scent and freedom of blooming of 'Prima Ballerina', but fortunately not the latter's propensity to be covered from head to foot in mildew spores by mid-July. Silvery-pink is the colour, and the moderately full blooms hold their high-centred form well as the outer petals reflex. It is one of the strongest-growing of the climbers in this book, making 3.7m (12ft). There is a tendency to become rather bare at the base if care is not exercised in keeping the shoots trained

as near to the horizontal as possible. It may be necessary to cut one or two of the main shoots back hard every so often to encourage new growth low down, but apart from this one reservation this is a fine rose.

Soldier Boy Le Grice, 1953. Seedling × 'Guinée'
Primarily a pillar rose that will climb to 2.4–3m (8–10ft) with a fine show of dazzling scarlet, single blooms early on and intermittent flowering later. In its colour a hard rose to beat and it has dark green, healthy leaves as well.

Sombreuil Robert, 1850. 'Gigantesque' seedling
A climbing sport of the bush form. An early Tea rose of great beauty with large, flat, many-petalled, quartered blooms, creamy-white with a hint of pink in the centre. In flower over a long period, but do not expect a tremendous flush of bloom, or even two flushes. There will be, rather, a non-stop but quietly restrained display, which will be every bit as impressive in its own way. A fine Tea rose scent and good foliage.

Sparkling Scarlet Meilland, 1970. 'Danse des Sylphes' × 'Zambra'
A climber that is far better known on the continent of Europe than it is in the United Kingdom, a situation that should be rectified. It is a rose of medium vigour, which means that it will climb to about 3m (10ft), but it branches well so that whatever it is trained against will be well covered. It is, in fact, suitable for most situations, and it will light them up with its clusters of rather small, semi-double, bright red blooms. A good second showing in the autumn and healthy, bright green leaves.

Summer Wine Kordes, 1984. 'Coral Dawn' × seedling of 'Zitronenfalter'
The large, single blooms are coral-pink, shading to yellow in the centre, where the red anthers are well displayed. It is fully remontant, but carries a succession of high-quality blooms rather than concentrating on spectacular flushes. Quite a strong grower, it will reach 3.7m (12ft) and be well covered with light green, semi-glossy leaves that seem to darken in colour with age. A very promising rose that is being stocked by more nurseries each year and one that would have received more marks from me if only it had a stronger fragrance.

White Cockade Cocker, 1968. 'New Dawn' × 'Circus'
A climber that might have been designed for the smallest gardens of all. In fact it is sometimes referred to as a semi-climber, for it will seldom go much over 2.1m (7ft), but at that height it will be well covered with its fine, glossy foliage right to ground level and bear two good flushes of its shapely, white flowers. After a while these open wide to show their amber stamens. Not surprisingly, it can also be grown as a shrub.

1 Rosmarin

2 Officinalis

3 Bright Smile

4 Marjorie Fair

5 Essex

6 Joseph's Coat

7 Starina

8 Judy Fischer

9 Surrey

10 Dublin Bay

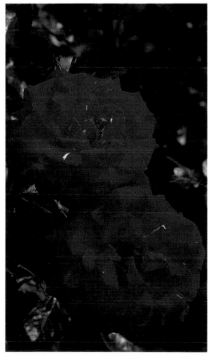

11 Fiona

12 Bonica

13 Zepherine Drouhin

14 Fire Princess

15 Stacey Sue

16 Goldfinch

17 Happy Thoughts

18 Helen Knight   *19 Rosa Mundi*

20 Trumpeter

Zéphirine Drouhin Bizot, 1868. Parentage uncertain, but classed as a Bourbon

Still, after all these years, one of the most widely grown of climbers despite being attacked by mildew almost every year. Clearly its reputation for being thornless has given it a great start over other roses and it is a very good variety in other ways, too. It is vigorous and freely branching and will probably climb to 3m (10ft) or so, though it will take a while to reach this height. The semi-double flowers, of a strong cerise-pink, are shapely at first but open quite loosely. They are carried with great freedom from midsummer until well into the autumn and have a fine fragrance.

CHAPTER 6

CHOOSING AND BUYING

The sheer number of new roses—and for that matter old roses—there are on the market makes it very difficult to choose which varieties to grow. A book or magazine article can tell you a good deal about some of them, but inevitably the choice of varieties will be based to a large extent on a particular author's preferences and on knowledge gained from his own experience of them. However, although such books (and this is one of them, of course) can be very helpful, they cannot cater for anyone's special tastes, other than those of the writer. Each individual has his or her particular likes and, as has already been emphasised, the only really satisfactory place to make a decision about the roses to buy is in a garden where you have seen them growing, preferably over a full season. Only in this way can you assess their true colour, their health, their ultimate size and bulk (of prime importance in a small garden), their weather resistance, whether or not their colour fades, whether they drop their petals cleanly when the blooms are fading, how quickly the flowers come again after the first flush and so on. Gardens do exist all over the country where a wide range of roses is displayed, and where they are also likely to be labelled. That of The Royal National Rose Society near St Albans in Hertfordshire, the Royal Horticultural Society's Wisley Garden in Surrey, Hyde Hall in Essex, Queen Mary's Garden in Regent's Park in London, and many of the National Trust gardens all over the country are all likely to be helpful, and some of the larger nurseries have display gardens of their own. In these the roses they sell are shown as mature plants, as you would see them in your own garden, and not in the immature stage that you would see if you made your choice from the nursery fields. If you can, it is as well to visit a garden reasonably close to where you live so that climate, soil and growing conditions in general are duplicated as closely as possible.

Circumstances (other than impatience, which should not be allowed to influence the matter) may render it impossible for you to visit such a show garden so that you have to make your choice in other ways. If this is so, do not use a rose show as a substitute, although you may see a wide range of varieties on display. They may look marvellous, but this is likely to be because they have been cossetted and protected from the weather for weeks before the show. They may, in fact, come from plants which produce only half-a-dozen good blooms a year, or from others the flowers of which, pristine when you see them, if not grown beneath individual bloom-protectors, become like lumps of sodden paper tissues after a light sprinkle of rain. Many of the varieties are grown for showing only, and are quite useless in the garden.

Catalogues from a good grower can be very useful for the undecided, but colour pictures, due to the unpredictability of both colour photography and colour printing, can produce some surprising results. Red roses and those with purple tints are particularly difficult to depict accurately and, while more colour correction in the printing would help, there simply is not the time or the money to carry this out. It can be, however, that the customer is misled because he wants to be! If a nursery shows the full truss of a Floribunda in its catalogue the customer, it has been found, will show little interest. However, if just one or two blooms of the rose are shown, making it look just like a Hybrid Tea, the orders will come flooding in. Strange, but there it is.

The fact that few catalogues comment on the health of a variety, even though it may be pretty generally known to be far from disease-free, is sometimes commented on adversely, but a moment's thought should provide an explanation. A certain variety may be white with mildew in one part of the country by the end of June, but be completely clear of it elsewhere. This can even happen in different parts of the same garden, though I suppose it is less likely in a small one. And so, as nurseries are in business to sell their roses, they can hardly be expected to tell everyone, in whatever part of the country they live, that a rose will get mildew if in most places it will not. They may even be unaware that a certain rose does not do well in a particular county or district.

However, if you go to a reputable nursery you should be well served, and you can always complain if you get a poor plant or the wrong variety. Most leading nurseries will replace such roses without quibble provided that you do not leave the matter too long. But how can you tell if you are getting a poor plant?

The British Standards Institution (and in America, The American Association of Nurserymen) have come up each with their own specification of a minimum standard, and they do not differ very much in their ideas. The British Standard states that the neck of the rootstock should be a minimum of 15mm (5/8in) in thickness (about as thick as your thumb), the root system should be well developed and fibrous, and that there should be at least two firm canes of at least the thickness of a pencil. Climbers should have two canes at least 75cm (30in) long, and standard roses should have two budding unions at the top of each stem, one each side so that a properly balanced head can be achieved. The main difference in the American specification is that the length of the canes is also given for bush roses and there are three overall grades. A good nursery will aim to better these minimum requirements, but nobody is entitled by law to market roses described as first grade if the BSI standards are not met.

These standards apply equally wherever you buy your roses, be it a nursery, store or supermarket, though more often than not pre-packed roses are not described as first grade. This is not surprising when one sees the quality of all too many of them, but it is quite possible to get good roses in this way if you know what to look for and you buy when they first appear in the store. All too often the storage conditions are too hot and dry and the plants, in their plastic bags, react as though they were in a greenhouse. They burst into premature growth with white, worm-like shoots, or else they become dried up and wrinkled. The price may be low, but one is taking a considerable chance in buying them—and not only because of their condition. One still sees on sale indifferent varieties that have long vanished from the nursery lists, and presumably they must be there only because they are easy to propagate from and there will be no royalty to pay on sales as there might be with more modern varieties. Buy by all means if you feel confident that you know what you are doing, but do not be too disappointed if the gamble does not come off.

It is, of course, almost impossible to examine the roots of pre-packed roses, and it would take a brave person to insist on having them all unwrapped in a crowded supermarket. This is another reason for caution, and the same general strictures apply to offers of cheap roses through the columns of newspapers. As in all transactions, one gets what one pays for. A guarantee to grow and bloom can be interpreted in many ways, but in fact you will not find many of the roses mentioned in this book at this cheaper end of the market.

An ever-increasing number of roses is being bought as container grown plants, which have the advantage that they can be put in the ground at almost any time. However, there are certain pitfalls for the unwary in buying roses in this way. It is all too easy to be swept off your feet by a showy spray of flowers on a container rose and to forget to look at the plant underneath, which might only have one, half-starved-looking stem. Because roses, even of the same variety, vary considerably in size, and the containers into which they are put (which are on the small side for ease of handling), do not, there is a tendency by the seller to pick the rose plants that will fit the containers rather than those that are the biggest and best. This is not to say that they may not meet the minimum standard already discussed, but they are less likely than other roses to exceed it.

They must for really satisfactory results have been actually grown in their containers and not be unsold stock from the previous season with its roots chopped off and crammed into a pot for quick sale. A reliable nursery would not, of course, do this, but not all qualify for a horticultural halo. Moss on the surface of the compost, or roots just emerging from the bottom holes in the pot, indicate that the rose has been in it some time, and one can always ask if there is any doubt.

Because preparing them is labour-intensive (which is why they are more expensive), the range of varieties on sale in containers tends to be rather limited, though this is gradually changing as people become more aware of the beauties they have been missing. At present, container plants are primarily for people who will buy them on impulse, rather than for those with definite ideas of what they want. For the latter, a nursery is the answer—and bare-root roses; but do not leave your ordering until the autumn when the roses you want may be sold out. Order early and both you and the nursery will be happy, and what could be nicer than that? Buying roses should be an exciting, enjoyable pastime and most of the leading rose growers try to ensure that it is just that for their customers. If I have, maybe, over-emphasised some of the pitfalls (for most of them will never occur if a little common sense is exercised), it cannot be bad, I think, to know what they are.

CHAPTER 7

PLANTING AND CULTIVATION

Before discussing planting, it would be useful to say a little about the setting of the rosebeds. By this I do not mean their placing in the garden, which may well be dictated by what is possible rather than what is ideal; but what might be called the framing of the beds.

Grass paths surrounding rosebeds always look well provided that the edges are kept neat and tidy. The green of the grass always blends happily with any other colour in the garden which, considering how much there is of it, is just as well. However, the greys and blue-greys of paving stones, both natural stone and many of the reconstituted kinds, are equally good for bordering beds, as are the honey-coloured paving slabs so reminiscent of the building in the Cotswold hills. They need the minimum of maintenance and, depending on how they are laid, may not even need weeds removed from between them. In wet weather, too, paving stones are a blessing, for the water quickly drains away. They last pretty well for ever.

If you decide to use paving, and on a patio there may be little choice, thought should be given not only to the colours of the slabs, but also to the pattern in which they are laid. Is it to be formal with the paving stones of uniform shape and size, or are they to be of random sizes or possibly crazy paving making use of broken pieces? To my mind, formality is for the surrounds of conventional borders of bedding roses, but for the informal kinds of rose we are primarily dealing with in this book, a more casual approach is much to be preferred. All the paving stones should be of one colour and no attempt made to create patterns, even if different tones of the same basic colour are used.

What about gravel paths to surround rose beds? Gravel can certainly look well, particularly if care is taken in choosing the right colour, but gravel is not for those who like an easy life. Even if the base on which it is laid is properly made it will gradually sink from view and have to be topped up, particularly on light, sandy soils, and it will constantly need weeding after the first year. It will really need some form of edging to keep it from wandering on to the beds.

An alternative to grass, paving or gravel is brick, but only if it is possible to get hold of second-hand ones that are ready mellowed, or else one is prepared to pay rather over the odds for ones which have been made especially to appear old. These will look very well, especially if your garden already has old brick walls or other brick-built structures. Unless you have a professional's skill, get a professional to do the laying. If inadequately laid, the path will very soon become uneven and the edges of the bricks will chip and crack. A really thick cement bed and good pointing is an absolute necessity.

Planting

Planting roses in a small garden is just the same as planting them anywhere else, except for a greater emphasis on container planting for patios and other paved areas and for the special requirements of miniature roses if one is to get the best out of them. However, wherever you garden, probably the most important thing of all is the proper preparation of the soil. Your roses will be in their new home for a very long time and giving them the best possible send-off makes a lot of sense. It is rare for the best of soils to be there for the asking. Most people have to try to improve what they have got and Dean Hole (who was founder and first President of The Royal National Rose Society), put it very well in one of his books:

> Look over your garden wall with a beautiful Rose in your coat, and your neighbour, loitering with his hands in his pockets, knee-deep in groundsel, and his beds undug, undrained, will sigh from the depths of his divine despair, 'What a soil yours is for the Rose!'

Unless it be pure sand or pure chalk, you cannot really tell what your soil may be like just by looking at it. That, for many people will be that and they will bother no further, realising that roses are adaptable plants. However, there are few soils that cannot be improved and it really is worth while taking a little trouble, at least in finding out whether your soil is acid or alkaline. For roses it should be slightly on the acid side or a reading of 6.5 on the pH scale. There are many cheap soil testing kits on the market which are very simple to use, and if a test is carried out and shows that your soil is very acid (a reading much higher than 6.5), it may be tempting to give the beds a dressing of lime. However, this is all too easy to overdo, and lime is virtually impossible to get rid of if you have done so. You will have a more or less permanent yellowing of the leaves of your roses caused by something called chlorosis, which means that the plant roots are unable to take up the iron salts they need from the soil. They have become insoluble or, as the text books rather quaintly put it, 'locked up'. Sequestered iron, sold in solution or in powdered form and applied to the beds, will help to counter this, but at a cost.

Calcium sulphate is the stuff to use at the rate of $90gm/m^2$ (2lb/sq yd) on heavy clay soils to improve the structure and it does not increase the alkalinity. Nitro-chalk will increase it a little and it contains sulphate of ammonia and nitrate of soda, making it a fertiliser as well as a soil conditioner. Peat will increase acidity if this is necessary and will help to improve the soil structure, but it will provide no plant foods. Additional plant fertiliser must be used with peat, and even if well-rotted garden compost or well-rotted stable manure be used instead, some additional bonemeal will not come amiss. To use another piece of horticultural jargon, roses are gross feeders.

It is best to begin your soil preparation about three months before you expect your new roses to arrive. The soil will then have time to settle down, any air pockets in it will have filled in, and the organic matter you have incorporated will have begun to break down and release some of the nutrients it is to provide for the roses. It will, of course, be disturbed again in the actual planting but only minimally and you will be treading it firm again after you have filled in the planting holes.

It is most desirable, particularly on light sandy soils, to add humus. This is basically made up of well-decayed vegetable matter which will, as has already been said, help to break up heavy soils, but it will also hold water and will encourage the bacterial action that is part of the yearly cycle that is necessary for plant growth. It will make the earth darker in colour, enabling it to heat up more quickly and retain its heat for longer periods, and in every way is a good and desirable thing. The ideal humus is well-rotted farmyard or stable manure, for it contains many plant foods in addition to its function as a soil conditioner. It is, however, by no means easy to get nowadays and, provided it has been properly made, well-rotted garden compost is a good second choice—if you can make enough of it. This is by no means simple to do in a small garden for there is seldom sufficient waste vegetable matter to make it from, and the only alternative is to buy in ready prepared humus-forming material. There are plenty of kinds on the market, but it is an expensive way of going about it.

If you do manage to make a reasonable amount of compost ensure that it is really ready before you use it. It should be rich, dark and crumbly. If it is not ready it will have to continue the breaking-down process after being incorporated in the soil, which will use up nitrogen at a great rate and take it from the roses.

Make sure, as far as is humanly possible, that all the worst perennial weeds have been removed from a new rosebed before planting commences. In the winter months many of them may be lurking out of sight beneath the soil, but digging should bring most of the roots to light.

Otherwise, once these have woven their way into and around the rose roots, they will be with you for ever more.

It is a myth that is a long time in dying—like the one about roses being not grown with other plants—that roses prefer a clay soil. They like a soil that is well drained but at the same time will retain a certain amount of moisture. This may sound like a contradiction, but a good medium loam will achieve this and is the ideal soil for roses. They will, however, do well in certain sorts of clay, which will hold water, but not in the kinds that become waterlogged. These, if they are to grow roses, will certainly need double digging to improve drainage, with manure, compost or coarse horticultural peat dug freely into the top spit, together with liberal helpings of bonemeal and hoof and horn meal, or else superphosphate or basic slag. Double digging should not be needed on light or medium soils. Only the top spit will need attention and the incorporation into it of humus and fertilisers.

Roses, though tolerant of most soils, do not thrive on chalk, though some of the old garden roses seem to be able to cope with it better than the more modern kinds. As a general policy, however, if you find yourself with a garden with solid chalk just beneath a thin layer of earth you must, if you wish to grow roses, dig out the chalk to a depth of at least 45cm (18in) and add plenty of peat to the soil with which you replace it. Otherwise chlorosis will follow with the yellowing of the leaves and the gradual weakening of the plants which follows this. Do not be tempted, as is sometimes advised, to line your planting holes with polythene, pierced with a fork for drainage. The holes will almost inevitably become blocked and before long the rose roots will be standing in water, which they will dislike just as much as they would have disliked the chalk. Reluctant as I am to discourage anyone from growing roses, I must advise in all honesty that, if you have a really chalky soil, grow the old garden roses by all means, but you would do better to keep your modern varieties in tubs and troughs.

It is also regrettable but true that, if you try to grow new roses in an old rosebed, they will not flourish. In the old bed the soil will almost certainly have become what is known as 'rose sick', which is a pretty all-embracing term first invented as far as I can see to describe something that nobody understood and so could not name properly. It was not a phenomenon confined to roses. With other plants such as conifers and fruit trees it was referred to as replant disease, but the result was the same, and even now the explanation is by no means certain. However, it is believed that organisms develop in the soil over the years which will attack the delicate feeding roots of newly planted roses but which cannot harm the tough old roots of long-established ones. This would certainly explain the fact that old roses will continue to grow happily in soil which will cripple new ones.

In a small garden, the question as to what can be done about an old rosebed if the roses need renewing is one of considerable moment, for there may not be room to make a new bed somewhere else. Changing the soil completely is one answer but, apart from the back-breaking work involved, where, in a small garden, is the new soil coming from? Buying it could be an expense not many people would want to be saddled with, to say nothing of all the labour involved.

The odd rose or two can be replaced easily enough by digging out a hole about 60cm–1m (2–3ft) wide by 45cm (1½ft) deep and replacing the soil in that, but if the replanting is to be more extensive, the only answer—assuming that moving the bed is impossible—is soil sterilisation. This can be a time-consuming and messy business, especially if formaldehyde is used, which is about the only soil steriliser left that the ordinary gardener is allowed to use under the latest regulations. However, it is always possible and should not be too costly to bring in a gardening contractor to carry out the work with a chemical such as basimid. This has to be dug into the ground, which must then be covered up with black polythene for about ten days to keep in the gases which are released and which fumigate the soil. Rather unsightly, but not really for very long.

If you decide in the end to move your rosebed to another spot, the old one will be quite all right to grow other plants in.

Any time during the winter or early spring is suitable for planting roses provided that there is no frost about. The traditional month is November and, as so often with traditional gardening ways, it is probably the best one. Nurseries usually aim to get their roses to you in November or thereabouts, for this is the time when the soil is still relatively warm and the roses can even put out a few new roots before going to sleep for the winter. However, no harm should come to them if rose bushes are planted at any time up to the end of March. They will simply be rather later in getting away and may be more susceptible to the droughts that often occur in the spring but go unnoticed because the sun is not shining. Roses planted in the spring should be more than usually carefully watered.

If new roses arrive from a nursery when there is frost about, or they cannot be planted immediately for some other reason, they will be perfectly happy if left, unpacked, in a cool though frost-proof shed. Do not keep them in the house, for heat is the last thing they need. If the delay is likely to be more than a few days, heel the roses in in a trench in a spare corner of the garden, but do plant them properly as soon as possible. They are incredibly tough and will put up with treatment that would kill many other plants, but this should not be taken advantage of.

As the rosebed will have been already prepared, the planting holes can now be dug. How far apart they should be must depend on the size and growth habit of the roses you are planting. A number of those recommended in this book will spread out far more widely than the average Floribunda or Hybrid Tea and the distances to which they are likely to aspire are given in the text, especially where they are exceptional. No average can be given as it can with more conventional roses.

The planting holes should be deep enough for the budding unions to be about 3cm (1in) below soil level and wide enough for the roots to be well spread out. After digging them a planting mixture can be prepared which will go into the planting holes mixed in with ordinary soil and help to get the roses off to a good start, like porridge for breakfast on a cold morning. About half a bucketful per rose of soil and fine peat mixed fifty-fifty and with a small handful per rose of a slow-acting fertiliser such as bonemeal well stirred in will do very well, and can be mixed and taken to the planting site in a wheelbarrow.

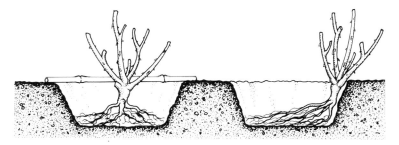

13 Planting a patio or shrub rose

When all this is ready, unpack the roses and inspect them for broken shoots or roots, which should be cut away. Cut away, too, any shoots showing signs of disease, though roses from a reputable nursery should have none of these. Shorten long, thick, thong-like roots by about a half, which will encourage the production of fine feeding roots instead. If the roses look rather dried out, exercise a little patience and soak them in a bucket of water for an hour or so. Take them to the planting site wrapped in damp sacking so that they cannot dry out again.

I have more than once seen it suggested that the earth in the centre of the planting hole should be mounded up a little and the roots of the rose arranged neatly, radiating out from this central mound. This is the advice of someone who has never planted a rose and would make excellent sense if rose roots grew like that. But they do not, and all you can do is to place a rose in its planting hole, check that it is at the right level by putting a cane across the hole, and try to spread the self-willed roots out as evenly as possible. All of which can be rather like trying to put a reluctant cat into a cat basket, a situation not made any easier by the modern mechanical method of planting the rootstocks. This results in the roots all pointing in one direction and, if this is what you find, the rose must be planted against one side of the planting hole and the roots fanned out over the rest of it. Then, holding the rose in place with your third hand, tip in the planting mixture and the surrounding soil, firming it with the toe rather than the more drastic heel of your boot or shoe. Firm planting is important, but care must be taken, especially if you garden on heavy soil, that it is not compacted so that rain cannot penetrate.

When the roses are in, water them well and, if planting after the turn of the year, pruning should be done at once. With a new rose, this should be drastic. It takes courage to cut something for which you have paid good money down to 5–8cm (2–3in) above the ground, but that is what should be done so that new roots can be forming before the growing strength is switched to the top-growth. Firm the plants again after a few weeks and yet again after a frosty spell in winter, as this can loosen them in the soil.

CONTAINER GROWN ROSES can, of course, be planted at almost any time, the exceptions being during a hard frost and during a drought. It is not, however, enough just to make a hole the same size as the container, take the rose out of the latter, and then push it into the hole. The ground around the planting hole should be properly broken up and fertiliser added, just as it would be with any other kind of rose, for its requirements are exactly the same. If this is not done, the roots of the rose may never spread out properly, and the planting hole, especially in heavy soils, may simply collect water, in which the rose roots will not be happy.

Before planting, soak the roses in their containers to make sure that they do not go dry into the planting hole. If they are in a peat-based compost and they do go in dry, it may be difficult to get them to take up water later. Put the first rose into its planting hole and, if the container is of black polythene, slit it down the sides and ease it out from under the rootball, trying as far as possible to keep the latter intact, though it will pay to loosen the sides a little. This should also be done if the rose comes out of a plastic flowerpot in order to increase the contact between the roots and the soil. In either case, once the rose is in its hole, check the planting depth and, if this is correct, fill in round the sides of the rootball with planting mixture and soil.

CLIMBERS if planted against the wall of a house will be in very dry soil or else may have water dripping on them for long periods from the eaves, neither of which condition they will like. So make sure that they are not in line with the edges of the eaves and that you position the planting holes at least 45cm (18in) away from the wall. Slope the rose shoots in towards it and the roots in the planting hole away from it towards moister soil.

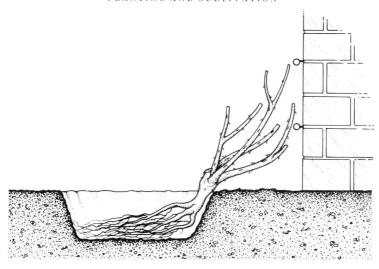

14 Planting a climbing rose against a wall

HEDGES that consist of small, narrow and very upright varieties are best if the bushes are planted in two rows, staggered and about 45cm (18in) apart.

STANDARD ROSES always need a strong stake put into the planting hole to support them, weeping standards needing a longer and stronger stake than ordinary ones as the head will be bigger and the stem longer. This should be driven into the centre of the planting hole before the rose is put in. If done afterwards it might well damage some of the roots and even cause suckers, to which the usual Rugosa understock of standard roses is rather prone. To help keep these down, shallow planting is essential and the soil mark on the stem as it came from the nursery should be strictly adhered to when deciding planting depth. The stake should come just up to the budding union and not beyond. One plastic tie with a buffer incorporated between the rose and the stake should be attached about 30cm (1ft) above the ground and a second just below the head. With weeping standards an extra one in the middle would not come amiss. Do not tighten any of them up until the rose has had time to settle in the earth or there is a risk that it might be left suspended. When the ties are eventually tightened, remember to allow room for expansion of the stem.

GROWING IN TUBS OR TROUGHS does not differ too greatly from growing roses anywhere else, and as a growing medium any good potting compost that does not dry out too quickly, such as John Innes No2 or No3 would be suitable. The right containers are one of the most important considerations, but whether they be made of stone, plastic, fibreglass or wood is a matter of personal taste. They must, however, be large enough to do their job properly, which means large enough to give the roses a good root-run with a minimum depth of 45cm (18in) for full-sized roses and 23–25cm (9–10in) for miniatures. They must have good drainage holes and should be stood on blocks so that surplus water can run away freely. A layer of crocks should be placed in the bottom of the container before the compost goes in.

The containers should be placed in a sunny spot where they cannot be dripped on by overhanging trees or shrubs. Water well in dry weather and feed the roses twice a year just as one would roses growing in a border. Every second year, scrape some of the compost from the top of the container and replace it with new. If the chosen containers are large — perhaps half-barrels — and there is a likelihood of their having to be moved every so often, it may be better to use a peat-based compost. This will be considerably lighter, but watering in hot spells will have to be carried out more frequently.

Fertilisers

If you have prepared your rosebed in the way described at the beginning of this chapter you will have got your roses off to an excellent start, but just the same they will use up the foods you have provided with almost indecent haste. In light soils, too, many of the essential salts will be washed away by rain and must be replaced. Nitrogen, which stimulates growth of the leaves and shoots (and the lack of which is indicated by the yellowing of leaves and small, anaemic flowers), phosphates, which speed up flower production and help the roots to grow (and lack of which may mean dull green leaves, weak stems and flower buds not opening), and potash, which gives resistance to drought and disease and good growth and flowers (and lack of which turns leaf margins yellow and then brown, coupled with a general lack of vigour), are the three most important rose foods. To these must be added calcium and magnesium and a number of other chemicals known as trace elements for the very good reason that their quantities are so small as to constitute only a trace in each case. Unless your roses indicate an especial lack of any of these in the soil, a balanced proprietary rose fertiliser is all you will need.

Always use gloves when handling fertilisers or any other chemical product, even though the experts on television programmes never do. This is not an alarmist doctrine, but common sense when one considers how little we really seem to know about their long-term effect. A small handful of one of the proprietary fertilisers sprinkled around each rose bush and lightly hoed in shortly after pruning and again in July before the second flush of bloom gets going should be all that is needed. Do not put fertiliser on later than this as it would only encourage the production of autumn growth that will not have time to ripen before the frosts of winter arrive to kill it off. If you wish to help in the speedy ripening of shoots that do come late and so minimise their loss, a slightly later dressing of sulphate of potash at 75gm/m^2 (2oz/sq yd) will help, but if you stick to the July date for the last of the fertiliser there should really be no problems.

Foliar feeding, in which the fertiliser is sprayed straight on to the leaves and stems of the plant so that it is absorbed straight into the system, by-passing the roots, is something of a luxury in the average garden. It can, however, have advantages in certain cases, where the soil is very alkaline, for instance, as it may help to overcome the effects of chlorosis, or if there is a drought, when lack of liquid in the soil will make it much more difficult for plant foods to be absorbed. The leaves of roses will show the benefits of foliar feeding almost immediately and will be remarkable for their size. For this kind of feeding, use a proprietary feed mixed according to the maker's instructions and spray it on to the leaves, preferably early in the morning before the sun has any real heat in it. Some foliar feeds can also be used as liquid fertilisers to be watered on the soil, which can be useful if quick results are needed, but the slow-acting fertiliser mentioned earlier is more satisfactory in the long run and lasts for months rather than weeks.

Plant problems

From time to time your roses, or an odd plant or two among them, may show signs that all is not well. This may be due to disease or attack by insects, which will be dealt with shortly, but if it is due to a soil deficiency, here are some of the symptoms and possible causes. It should be stressed, however, that the symptoms of one deficiency are sometimes so like the symptoms of another that it is by no means always easy to put your finger on what is wrong. Very often a straight dose of a general fertiliser is all that is needed to put things right and this is always worth trying first.

1) *Young leaves pale green with stems weak and stunted and possibly with red tints*	Shortage of nitrogen. Apply Sequestrene and avoid liming.
2) *Oldest leaves show yellow between the veins*	Shortage of manganese. Spray with 25g (1oz) manganese sulphate in 4.5 litres (1gal) of water and avoid liming.

3) *Young shoots die back and brown spots form around leaf edges*	Shortage of calcium. Use a proprietary rose fertiliser.
4) *Leaves very dark green and possibly misshapen*	Shortage of boron. Use a proprietary rose fertiliser.
5) *Yellow areas on leaves, which may become entirely yellowed*	Shortage of iron. Apply Sequestrene as described earlier.
6) *Oldest leaves pale green and yellow between main veins. They drop early*	Shortage of magnesium. Use a proprietary rose fertiliser.
7) *Brown, brittle edges to the leaves. Buds may fail to open*	Shortage of potassium. Apply a good general fertiliser.
8) *Young leaves small, dark green and purplish-green underneath. Stems stunted and weak*	Shortage of phosphorus. Apply good general fertiliser.

All this may sound very daunting but, as has been said earlier on, a general fertiliser will cure most of the ills. In fact, unless you have very peculiar soil indeed, you will probably not have to take any special steps at all. The odd rose may show signs of what looks like a particular deficiency, but will have fully recovered by the next season of its own accord. It is really only if a whole rosebed looks sick that thought must be given to taking more drastic measures.

Mulching

In late spring when the soil has, or should have, started to warm up the time for mulching has arrived. This means spreading over the surface of the beds a layer of material, preferably organic, about 5–8cm (2–3in) thick. This should only be done when the soil is moist as part of the function of a mulch is to stop evaporation from the soil surface and so keep the water in. It will also smother the majority of weeds, though it is best to remove the tougher perennial ones before the mulch goes on. The best mulch of all, stable manure, will eventually break down into humus and provide plant foods. Finally, a mulch will help to keep the soil temperature more or less even.

A very wide range of materials has been tried as a mulch. Compost will, when broken down, provide plant foods like manure, but it can contain weed seeds and look a bit untidy. The latter objection also applies to leaf-mould, and from the point of view of appearance, if not of cheapness, peat and chipped forest bark are hard to beat. Grass cuttings should only be used with discretion because, if they are applied too thickly, they can form a mat which the rain finds difficult to penetrate. In autumn the mulch can be lightly hoed in when the beds are tidied up.

It is to be regretted that blackbirds and thrushes like mulches on the beds just as much as the roses do. In keeping the soil moist the mulch encourages worms, and scattering the mulch over the lawn surrounding the beds in order to get at these is a favourite pastime of the birds. Mulches and birds go together; you cannot have one without the other.

Dead-heading

The year by year life cycle of the rose—or, indeeed of any plant—is to grow from seed, to produce leaves and flowers, the latter being fertilised in due course so that more seed is formed. This falls to the ground, germinates, and the cycle starts once more. The seeds of the rose are

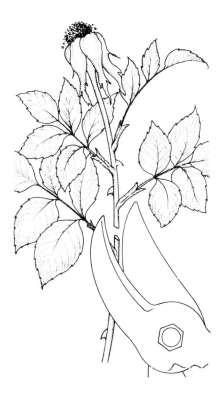

15 Dead-heading a rose bloom after flowering

contained in the hips and, if these are allowed to form, the cycle has been almost completed and there is no need for more flowers to be produced. However, a rose does not usually cut off flower production just like that. The blooms will just get fewer and fewer as the season progresses, so the removal of the dead flowers before the hips can form is necessary to keep them going. Once the hips have been taken away, the rose will have to try again and more flowers will be the result.

If, in dead-heading, you simply snap off the dead flowers, you will be left with the unsightly stumps which will eventually die back. Cutting the old flowering shoots back with secateurs to about the third bud down the stem, just as if you were carrying out a mini-pruning, is the best way to dead-head and will produce stronger new flowering shoots the second time round. Dead-heading, if performed regularly, is very little trouble, and can be done as you wander around the rosebeds of an evening; but do not make the mistake of dead-heading the varieties that have been grown especially for their display of hips! Apart from the fact that you will be depriving yourself of the display, they do not need this kind of treatment as the majority will be once-flowering kinds. An exception to this—and with roses there always are exceptions to any generalisation one tries to make—would be the Rugosa family, which will obligingly keep flowering and producing hips at one and the same time. Which is one of their attractions.

Suckers

Suckers are nowadays much less of a problem than they used to be, at any rate on new roses, which is largely due to the widespread use of an understock called Laxa, a form of the Dog Rose, *R. canina*. It is from the understock on to which a cultivated variety of rose is budded that suckers come, the stock being used to give qualities to the variety that it might not otherwise possess. Some stocks make a rose grow better on heavy soils, most give extra vigour, some are better for light soils, and so on. Laxa is better because it does not sucker much, but the choice of stock used is up to the nursery which grows the roses and each has its favourite. A rose will adapt to many conditions as has already been stressed, but if you do have soil that is, perhaps, exceptionally heavy, it might be as well to get your roses from a firm that uses *R. canina* itself as an understock.

If a sucker is allowed to grow, it—and its companions, which will soon branch out from it—will gradually take over the cultivated variety, robbing it of nourishment until it finally succumbs; so they must be removed promptly. This is easily said, but many people have difficulty in recognising a sucker and distinguishing it from a new shoot of the cultivated rose. Generally speaking, however, a careful examination will show that, not only is the sucker shoot a different colour (usually a much lighter green), but the thorns will be of a different shape as well. There may well be seven leaflets to each leaf instead of five, but this can only be taken as a useful pointer and one not to be regarded as foolproof. If there is any doubt at all, try to trace the sucker to its source, scraping some soil away from the base of the rose if necessary. If the suspect comes from below the budding union (the point from which the shoots radiate), from the roots, that is, it is certainly a sucker and should be pulled off, not cut. Cutting a sucker is the equivalent of pruning it and will encourage new growth. Pulling it away not only removes the sucker itself, but also removes dormant buds that may be lurking at its base.

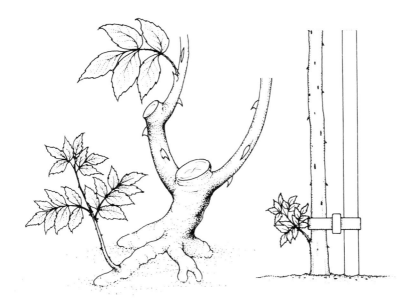

16 Removal of a sucker from (left) a shrub rose and (right) a standard rose

The stem of a standard rose is actually a shoot coming from the understock, to the top of which the cultivated variety is budded. So a shoot forming on the standard stem is actually a sucker and should be snapped off as soon as seen.

A rose grown on its own roots, as many miniatures are, will not, of course, produce suckers from a rootstock. All new shoots will be those of the variety, and the same point applies to roses grown by micro-propagation. It has always been held that many roses, particularly the Hybrid Teas and Floribundas, will not grow nearly so well on their own roots, and it has yet to be explained how this ties in with the prediction made so confidently nowadays that the future of rose breeding lies with micro-propagation.

Disbudding

Few of the roses described in this book will need disbudding. It means the removal, as soon as they are large enough to handle, of the sidebuds that surround the central one, particularly with Hybrid Teas. This allows all the growing strength of that shoot to go into the one flower that is left, which should end up as something rather special. This procedure is not usually necessary for garden display, though it is extensively used when exhibiting roses. So, too, is the practice of disbudding Floribundas by removing at an early stage the central flower of each truss. This accelerates the opening of the other buds, which will all open out at once. However, this is specialist treatment and quite needless for the average garden.

Pruning

This is something that causes more anguish than almost any other aspect of rose growing, but once one has mastered the basic principles one looks back and wonders why. If one considers just how a rose grows, what one has to do makes common sense. All roses send up new shoots that flower well the first year. If they are left alone they will flower slightly less well the second year and, as year by year they gradually deteriorate, so will the flowering become progressively less good. The blooms will be smaller and some of the shoots may have become diseased and discoloured and are clearly on their way out. However, at the same time as this is happening, new shoots will be growing from the base of the plant to take their place.

Pruning is simply an acceleration of this process, getting rid of the shoots which have flowered once before deterioration has set in and encouraging the strong new shoots which will take their place to form that little bit sooner. It also gets rid of thin, twiggy growth which would never produce flowers and of dead or diseased wood, and it will help to keep the bushes shapely by removing or shortening shoots that would have thrown it out of balance. Finally it can be used to open up the centre of a rose bush to allow proper air circulation — which will help to keep disease at bay — at the same time removing shoots that may be rubbing together. This can cause damage through which disease spores can enter the shoots.

These general principles apply to all roses, but when it comes down to detail, there are some differences in the pruning of the different families. At one end of the scale come the Hybrid Teas with which, as it happens, we are not much concerned in this book, and in which the size and quality of each flower is all-important. To achieve this the pruning should be much more severe than it is with any other rose, but exactly the opposite applies with the species roses. Much of their charm lies in their long, arching canes which will bear, year after year along their entire length, the most enchanting single flowers. Cutting back the shoots would largely destroy this effect, so only dead or diseased wood should be removed.

These are the two extremes, but there are many small variations in between, which makes it impossible to give one set of pruning instructions that will cover all kinds. That is why appropriate hints have been given in the descriptive notes in previous chapters. Here, only the general principles that apply to all rose pruning and the equipment needed are described.

First and foremost, buy the best pair of secateurs that you can afford. They will be strong and well designed, and they will last a lifetime if properly looked after. Some of the cheaper secateurs will bruise rose stems when making a cut, encouraging the entry of disease or of die-back.

Always keep your secateurs clean and sharp. Use methylated spirits to wipe them if they have been cutting into diseased wood to prevent the infection from being passed on. Very thick shoots or the woody stumps left from past prunings can be dealt with by a long-handled lopper or a fine-toothed pruning saw.

A cut shoot may show a brown centre, which means that die-back is spreading down the inside. If you come across this, cut again to a lower bud, and continue this until white wood is reached, even if it means going almost to ground level. If you do not do this the shoot will probably die right away and so vanish anyway. The usual injunction to cut to an outward-facing bud will only apply to a minority of the roses described in this book, for so many of them are low, spreading growers. The instruction really means cut to a bud facing in the direction you want a new shoot to develop, and with upstanding types like the Floribundas and Hybrid Teas, this would normally be outwards to encourage bushiness. With lax or wide-spreading roses the instruction might well be to cut to an upward or inward-facing bud to encourage upward rather than outward growth. Once again, it is a matter of common sense and of encouraging the rose to do what you want it to do.

Pruning should be less severe on poor, light soils, for there will be less for the plant to feed on to build itself up again. Prune newly planted roses much harder than established ones. This, as was mentioned in the last chapter, is to encourage the growth of a strong root system before energy is diverted into producing top-growth.

Advice about the right time of year to prune varies according to who is giving it, which indicates, as so often when experts differ, that there is no one answer and that roses can be pruned at any time when they are dormant or semi-dormant. In the United Kingdom, this means between November and March in the South and November and April in the north.

Autumn pruning will mean that the roses get away to an earlier start in the spring, which may or may not be a good thing, depending on the sort of weather conditions they have to cope with. And apart from that, if the winter is a severe one the pruned canes may be subject to considerable frost damage and have to be gone over again in the spring. So, bearing all these considerations in mind, the decision as to when you prune must be guided to some extent by how far north you live and also by the weather conditions in any particular year. If in doubt, stick to the traditional month of March for a spring prune and you will not go far wrong. Never, however, prune during a frosty spell or severe die-back may be the result.

Taking cuttings

Almost all the roses described in this book will take easily from cuttings. From my own observations, it would appear that the nearer a rose is to its wild ancestors, the easier it is to be successful with cuttings from it. Thus, what are perhaps the most highly developed roses of all, the Hybrid Teas, are the most tricky and unpredictable, whereas with ramblers and most shrub roses it would be very difficult to fail. Species take easily, but with them a word of warning is necessary. If grown on their own roots, as they would be if raised from cuttings, they are apt to make far too much top-growth at the expense of flowering.

A caution, too, is needed with some other groups of roses such as the Pimpinellifolia family, the Gallicas and Albas and one or two others if they are on their own roots. They will send out suckers freely, but these will not, of course come from a rootstock. They will come from the rose itself and, on light soils, will spread through the ground with quite incredible rapidity, popping up as new plants in what are often the most inconvenient places. Once established with a many-branched network of roots, they are extremely difficult to bring back under control. The Gallica 'Charles de Mills' has got away from me in my garden and, lovely rose that it is, one can have too much of it.

However, not all roses are so badly behaved and taking cuttings is a cheap and interesting way of increasing your stock. It will not, of course, give you new varieties, but more of what you have already is often welcome, for making a hedge from one original plant, for instance.

It is often said, as was mentioned earlier, that roses will not be as vigorous on their own roots as would be the same varieties when budded on to stocks. As stocks are used, at least in part, to increase vigour, there must be something in this argument, though stocks are used for other reasons, too, as we have seen. Although it is true that many of what one might call the more sophisticated roses such as the Hybrid Teas will be less happy on their own roots, but I have taken cuttings successfully from most rose families and have never been conscious of a marked lack of vigour in the resulting plants. In any case, it could be argued that, for the purposes of this book, small size is a very desirable quality!

It has already been mentioned in the chapter on miniature roses that this is one group which is grown from cuttings commercially with increasing frequency. Clearly the results are acceptable, and miniatures take easily and reach maturity quickly. Budding on such a small scale is a fiddly business and in the end produces plants that may be bigger than the dedicated miniature grower really wants.

In a climate such as that of the United Kingdom, there is no need for a frame or greenhouse or any form of special winter protection. Hardwood cuttings should be taken in early autumn, using shoots of your chosen roses that have flowered at midsummer and are about as thick as a pencil. Before cutting them, however, the cuttings bed should be got ready.

Choose a spot that is nice and open but at the same time sheltered from the mid-day sun. If your soil is on the heavy side, dig a narrow trench about 18cm (7in) deep and sprinkle 2.5cm (1in) of coarse sand along the bottom. The length of the trench will depend on how many cuttings you are planning to put into it, but reckon on their being about 13–15cm (5–6in) apart. They would grow happily a good deal closer than this, but the spacing suggested does allow for them, once they have become plants, to be removed from the cuttings bed one or two at a time with the minimum of root disturbance for the rest.

If you have light, sandy soil, a trench is probably unnecessary and even the sand can be omitted. All that is needed is a narrow slit in the soil of the same length as the trench, made by pushing a spade vertically 15cm (6in) into the ground along a centre line and working it back and forth. Your cuttings bed is now ready to receive your cuttings.

Any shoot of reasonable length should produce two or three cuttings of approximately 23cm (9in). Cut away the soft tip and divide the rest of the shoot, cutting with a sharp knife immediately above a leaf axil bud at the top and immediately below one at the bottom. Snap off the thorns (which should come away readily, leaving the bark undamaged) and remove all but the top two leaves from each cutting. (Some people hold that this is unnecessary and that they get just as good results with all the leaves stripped. My procedure is the time-honoured traditional one but maybe experiment has proved that the leaves need not be removed after all. I have not tried it, but probably will some day.)

Next moisten the ends of the cuttings and dip them in a hormone rooting powder, though once again it has been argued that they will root quite happily without its aid. This is probably true as I have in the past discovered that the rooting powder I was using was well past its shelf-life and probably quite inactive, but let us say that in using it one is taking out that little extra bit of insurance cover.

Tap off any excess powder and then insert the cuttings vertically into

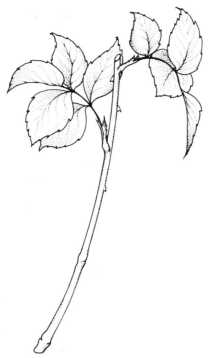

17 A cutting ready for planting

the trench or slit, leaving only about one-third of their length above ground. Tread them in firmly and water well. Keep them watered in dry spells and tread them in once more after a frost, which may have loosened them in the ground. They must be firm if they are to take properly.

It is likely that it will take a minimum of three years to produce a fully grown plant from a cutting, for the first year will largely be taken up with producing a good root system. There will usually be a few flower buds developing during the first summer and, tempting as it will be to see how these turn out, it is really better to remove them before the flowers form. Allow all the growing energy to be concentrated into developing a strong plant and not be diverted into decoration. It is preferable to leave rooted cuttings in place for two seasons before transplanting them to their final home in the garden. Otherwise they will be too small really to fill the space which they have been allocated and will merely look lost and woebegone.

CHAPTER 8

ROSE PESTS AND DISEASES

A great deal of attention is given to pests and diseases in the gardening press, and in advertisements for sprays and chemicals to combat them. However, it cannot be too strongly stressed that very few diseases and only one insect are of serious concern to the average grower of roses.

The diseases are black spot, mildew and, in some areas, rust. In many parts of the country they can be quite easily kept in check by spraying only as and when they are first seen, and in some years they may be almost completely absent. In others attacks may be frequent and several sprayings may be necessary, while there are certain areas where rust and black spot are endemic. In this case preventive spraying is probably called for at regular intervals, perhaps as often as every ten days.

However, the point I am making is that it is not necessary for everyone who grows roses to spray against either disease or insects regularly throughout the growing season. As with pruning, adapt to what you yourself find to be needed. In my own case, gardening in Surrey, I have found that on average I have to spray no more than twice or thrice a year to keep my roses free from disease, and I rarely, if ever, spray against insects. Greenfly, the only insect most people need worry about, come and go of their own accord and in some years hardly appear at all.

Spraying your roses is one of the most boring of gardening chores and the chemicals that make up the sprays get ever more expensive. In addition, there is a growing awareness that we still do not really know what the long-term effects of what we are doing may be, so for all these reasons the less we spray the better. After all, it is not so long ago that DDT was thought to be the answer to the insect menace but was subsequently found to cause more problems than it cured and was banned. The thing to work out is just how infrequently one has to spray, not how frequently.

The effectiveness of sprays has advanced rapidly in recent years and they can now be said to provide control if not a cure for the three main rose diseases. It was only as recently as 1989 that something became available on the retail market that would deal with rust, and was available

113

in the small quantities needed by the average gardener, but part of the problem, whether it be with sprays for diseases or insects, is that an immunity to their effectiveness can be built up surprisingly quickly. For this reason it is recommended that the kinds of spray used be varied. One highly respected nurseryman of my acquaintance varies the spray with every application, but I would suggest that a change half-way through the season would be enough for most people to cope with.

The introduction of systemic sprays has made life a great deal easier. These penetrate into the tissue of the plant so that they are not washed off by rain and stay effective for a number of weeks. However, most of them are not, as was once generally believed, carried by the sap to all parts of the plant. Most penetrate the surface but do not travel onwards, so when spraying make sure that all parts of a rose bush are wetted, the undersides of the leaves as well as the top surfaces. Never do more than wet the plants thoroughly. Drenching them so that the liquid spray pours off on to the ground is a waste of good money. Never spray in hot sunshine or you may cause leaf-scorch. The cool of the evening is best, but not so late that the leaves do not have a chance of drying off before darkness comes.

A number of sprays will kill the majority of harmful insects, while others will control both black spot and mildew. So-called cocktails are available with the whole lot mixed together and in theory this should be the ideal solution. One spraying and all troubles vanish like smoke, but in practice it has been found that it is best to keep the insecticides and fungicides separate. They seem to lose some of their effectiveness when combined, and you should never be tempted to mix any of them yourself. It can not only be dangerous, but is against the law.

The instructions on some spray bottles or packets advise their use at different strengths for different conditions. Follow these instructions but do not be tempted into experimenting with different strengths yourself. All kinds of damage to your roses might be the result.

Pest and disease remedies are also sold as powders, to be puffed on to plants from special puffer packs, but these are not really very practical unless you have very few roses or unless, perhaps, you want to treat half a dozen miniatures in a trough. In theory a thin layer of powder should settle on the leaves, but it is extremely difficult to get an even covering and quite impossible if the wind is blowing. Some of your roses are apt to look as if they had come straight out of a flour mill while others are scarcely touched. And rain will, of course, wash the powder straight off.

As a final word before getting down to specific details of the various pests and diseases, it should be stressed that all roses will be healthier and better able to shrug off attack by disease spores if they are well looked after in other ways. Strong plants are likely to be healthy plants.

Rose diseases

MILDEW The first signs will be grey, powdery-looking spots on the leaves and flower stems. The spores that cause mildew are airborne and will spread rapidly, in bad cases covering the whole plant (and its neighbours) and distorting growth. A whole bed of roses covered with mildew is a sorry sight, but it should never get to that stage with sprays available nowadays.

Dryness at the roots has been cited as one of the causes of mildew, but the incredibly hot, dry summers of 1976 and, more recently, 1989, were ones during which mildew was almost completely absent, so it looks as if there is still research needed. It is almost certain, though, that the spores of mildew (and of black spot) overwinter in crevices on the rose canes and in the soil surrounding the bushes. Clearing away dead leaves in autumn should remove a possible further source of trouble and a winter wash can only do good. It will, if nothing else, get rid of a number of insect eggs and other undesirable things.

BLACK SPOT More serious than mildew, which may disfigure a plant but seldom kill it. Black spot can, over several years, be fatal, for it can defoliate a plant and so weaken it, progressively more so each year. The older, lower leaves are likely to be the first to show the tell-tale signs, round black spots with fringed edges, which in most years will not be seen before midsummer. The spots grow rapidly in size and spread over most of the leaf, the rest of which yellows. Eventually the leaves drop to the ground, but not before the spores have spread rapidly to other roses, particularly in damp weather. There are a number of good sprays to give control, but none that will cure. The tedious job of picking off and burning affected leaves will help to prevent the disease spreading, as will cleaning up the beds in autumn.

ROSE RUST There are two stages in the development of a rose rust attack. First come the spring spores, which show as small, orange pustules on the top surfaces of the leaves. These are not particularly infective, unlike the spores of late summer. These again show as orange pustules, this time on the under surfaces of the leaves. They eventually turn black, in which form they overwinter.

In a bad attack the leaves quickly become discoloured and fall, so the plant is weakened as it is with black spot, though a good deal more rapidly. Fortunately (for those who live elsewhere) rose rust is confined to certain parts of the country, though there are signs that it is slowly spreading further afield.

115

As already mentioned, there is now a good control for rust on the market and it will also deal with mildew at the same time. The makers claim that it is equally effective against black spot, but tests carried out by the RNRS would seem to cast a doubt on this. Not proven should, I think, be the verdict.

These, then, are the three most serious diseases that may attack roses. The sprays to use against them are shown in the chart at the end of this chapter. Something about other possible rose diseases now follows, but none of them is likely to be particularly serious and the majority of people will probably not even realise that their roses have been affected by them—with the possible exception of die-back. However, some information about them can be of value, if only to be able to reassure oneself that they are nothing worse.

CANKER A brown, sunken area on a rose shoot with the edges swollen and rough. It may grow until the stem is completely encircled and dies. Usually caused by parasitic fungus spores entering as the result of a wound. Cut away the infected stem and disinfect your secateurs afterwards with methylated spirits.

CROWN GALL Rough, brownish-coloured swellings, usually near the bud union (the crown) or on the roots (where they cannot be seen and so are likely to remain untreated), caused by soil-borne bacteria. On the shoots the problem is not serious as the infected part can easily be cut out and the cut sealed with pruning paint. On the roots the effect can be more serious, as the plant's development can be hindered and the cause not revealed unless perhaps some soil is being scraped away from the roots while searching for the source of a sucker. If thus found, affected roots should be cut away in the same way as the shoots, and it would be as well to disinfect the surrounding soil with something like Jeyes Fluid or Bordeaux mixture. Crown gall does not, however, occur very often.

DIE-BACK This, on the other hand, occurs all too often, with some roses (particularly the yellow and orange varieties) much more prone to it than others. It is rarely fatal and can be caused by frost damage, wood not properly ripened in summer, canker or a deficiency of potash in the soil which retards ripening. Affected shoots gradually die back and turn brown, beginning at the tips and gradually spreading downwards. Sometimes the die-back will halt of its own accord at a bud, but at other times it will move right down a shoot. Cut out the affected parts as described in the last chapter.

PURPLE SPOTTING Not, in fact, a disease at all, though it looks rather like black spot. However, the spots are actually dark purple instead of black, are usually much smaller and do not have fringed edges. It is caused by a soil deficiency or bad drainage, and can usually be got rid of by the application of a balanced rose fertiliser.

ROSE ANTHRACNOSE This is a fungus disease which causes white spots with red rims on the leaves, sometimes with brown, raised pustules on the stems as well. The red soon turns to yellow and if untreated the leaves will fall. Cut away infected shoots and spray with a fungicide to get rid of any spores that might otherwise overwinter on other parts of the plant.

VIRUSES Strange and often quite attractive patterns occasionally occur on rose leaves, particularly on varieties that have originated in the USA, where viruses are much more common. These are nothing to worry about and the roses seem to carry on quite happily, virus or not.

Insect pests

GREENFLIES OR APHIDS It has already been emphasised that this is the only insect pest that will, in the normal run of things, be of much concern to the gardener. Aphids are tiny, soft-bodied, light green or sometimes gingery-brown insects that gather in large numbers on young shoots and leaves (sometimes spreading to the old ones as well), and suck the sap. If they are left undisturbed, growth will be distorted and flower buds may fail to open. They breed with incredible rapidity, not only laying eggs but giving birth to live young as well, which is having the best of both worlds with a vengeance. A sticky substance which they produce and which is attractive to ants, is known as honeydew. It will coat stems and leaves, which soon become covered with an unsightly black fungus known as sooty mould.

Aphids are not, as most gardeners will find out, confined to roses and many plants have their own type of aphid. All kinds behave in much the same way (except for those that attack the roots of plants) and all can appear at any time from early summer onwards. If you have only a few roses and can face up to it, they can be removed with the finger and thumb. With a bad attack, a systemic insecticide may have to be used, but on the other hand the aphids may, by the time you have got around to doing the spraying, have mysteriously vanished away. Though do not count on it.

ANTS Especially on sandy soil it sometimes happens that ants will build their nests among the roots of a rose, in which case it will probably wilt. They will not be attacking the rose directly, but rather loosening the soil. An ants' nest destroyer should be applied.

CAPSID BUGS Small, bright green insects which cause small, brown spots on the young leaves and buds, making them wither before opening. Use an insecticide.

CHAFERS AND OTHER BEETLES The cockchafer, the rose chafer and the garden chafer are beetles which will nibble rose anthers and petals, causing ragged blooms. The grubs of the chafers may also attack the rose roots. Beetles can be picked off by hand and destroyed (the choice of how you do this is up to you!), or else an insecticide may be employed. Disinfecting the ground is the only way of getting rid of the grubs if it is suspected that they are causing damage, but it can be a difficult procedure with plants in place. Fortunately such attacks are rare.

FROGHOPPERS (CUCKOO-SPIT) Small, greenish-yellow, sap-sucking insects which hide in blobs of foam, usually in the angle between two shoots or around leaf-axils. Small numbers can be picked off by hand, but otherwise the foam must be washed away before spraying can be done. Not usually a serious pest, but at their worst they can cause distorted or wilting shoots.

LEAF-CUTTER BEES Small bees that cut circular pieces out of rose leaves and use them to line their nest tunnels, which can be found in dry, earthy banks and between the stones of dry-stone walls. Rarely numerous enough to cause problems, though I have in recent years heard of one very serious though localised attack. Dusting the leaves with a powdered insecticide will deter them.

LEAFHOPPERS Tiny, yellowish-green, jumping, sap-sucking insects which cause white mottling of the leaves. Their white moulted skins can be seen on the undersides after an attack. If serious can cause defoliation. Use an insecticide.

LEAF-MINERS They cause white blisters on the leaves, roughly in chain formation. There is a grub in each blister, so the leaves should be picked off and burned.

LEAF-ROLLING SAWFLIES Tiny black flying insects that lay eggs in the leaf margins, at the same time injecting a toxin that causes the leaves to roll up longitudinally. This can be very disfiguring in a bad year and especially in gardens sheltered by trees where the air tends to be still. Once it has struck, there is nothing you can do to mitigate the damage and spraying at that stage will neither kill the grub inside the rolled-up leaf, nor cause it to unroll. All you can do is pick off the rolled up leaves and burn them, but a much earlier preventive spray should work.

ROSE SCALE Limpet-like scales in clusters, mainly on the old rose stems, hide insects which suck the sap, causing the stems to wilt. An old and effective remedy is to dab the scales with methylated spirits, but otherwise spray as indicated in the chart.

ROSE SLUGWORMS Greenish-yellow caterpillars with pale brown heads, which rather resemble tiny slugs. They graze on the leaf surfaces in early spring, leaving skeletonised patches, the affected areas soon turning brown.

SPIDER MITES (RED SPIDER) Mites so small that the eye can scarcely see them and which suck the sap from leaves, causing them to turn a brownish-bronze before they fall. Tiny webs can be seen on the under-sides. Especially active in hot, dry conditions and may thus attack a rose on a south wall during a sunny summer. Also a menace in greenhouses. Control very difficult as insecticides seem ineffective (they are, after all, spiders, not insects) but cold water sprays will discourage them and for greenhouses there is now a natural predator which can be used. It is called *Phytoseiulus persimilis*.

THRIPS Very small, brownish-yellow insects that suck sap and also rasp the petal edges of rose blooms at the bud stage, so that the flowers open discoloured and misshapen. Pale-coloured roses seem particularly susceptible to attack. Thrips revel in hot weather and are sometimes known as 'thunder flies'.

TORTRIX MOTHS AND OTHER CATERPILLARS These can eat holes in the leaves and they can be picked off by hand if not too numerous. The tortrix moth caterpillar hides in a rolled up leaf, the edges of which are held together by silken threads: those of the lackey moth spin silken tents for themselves and drape them about the rose bushes: the winter moth caterpillar sticks two leaves together and nibbles away between them, happily out of sight.

Now, having seen the full range of horrors that can attack your roses, you can forget about most of them. Many of them will never appear at all, some very seldom, and a very large proportion of the total can be dealt with by only one or two sprays. These are listed below, with the name of the main chemical ingredient in each spray given. This will always be found on the packet or bottle containing the spray. Where treatment does not involve spraying it will be found under the entry for a particular disease or pest.

Diseases	Treatment
Black spot and mildew	Spray with benomyl, carbendazim, triforine, bupirimate-triforine, thiophanate-methyl or fenarimol. Remove and burn affected leaves.
Rose rust	Spray with myclobutanil.

Insect pests	
Greenfly, froghoppers, leafhoppers, scale insects, thrips	Spray with dimethoate, malathion, fenitrothion or pirimiphos-methyl.
Caterpillars and beetles (including chafers)	Spray with fenitrothion, gamma HCH, permethrin or pirimiphos-methyl.
Leaf-rolling sawfly	Spray with fenitrothion late April and again early May, before any sign of attack.
Rose slugworms	Spray with malathion, permethrin or gamma HCH.

All the sprays so far described involve the use of chemicals, which many people nowadays feel is wrong. Unfortunately there are no organic preparations that will deal with the fungus diseases of roses such as mildew, black spot and rust, but there are several organic insecticides. These, while effective, do have one or two disadvantages. They depend on contact with the insects to work and so spraying must be very thorough if they are all to be treated, especially under the leaves. Secondly, their effectiveness does not last for very long, so that spraying must be done more frequently. They are harmless to most plants and animals, but not to fish.

There are two main organic insecticides.

NATURAL PYRETHRUM will control small caterpillars, aphids, thrips, leafhoppers, ants and beetles.

DERRIS will control aphids, rose sawflies, small caterpillars, thrips and, to some extent, red spider mites.

Both these insecticides are available in either spray or dust form, the latter in a puffer pack. How often you have to use them must depend on how often attacks by the insects you are dealing with recur.

CHAPTER 9

OTHER PLANTS
WITH ROSES

It has long been said, largely I suspect by those who have not really thought about it, that roses cannot be mixed with other plants. I have tried to track down the origin of this idea and have found that it goes back a long way, though not, I suspect, much before the coming of the Hybrid Tea in the 1860s. This coincided with the upsurge of the use of roses as decorative plants in gardens.

Since pagan times they had been grown, as had most other plants we now consider as decorative, for medicinal uses, all sorts of draughts and potions being prepared from their petals, hips and roots. Then, largely through the influence of the wife of Napoleon I, the Empress Josephine, and her rose collection at Malmaison outside Paris, the rose gradually began to be appreciated for the beauty of its flowers rather than for its more utilitarian functions as a natural storehouse of medicines. However, the kinds of roses that were then being grown were largely the big, informal shrubs like the Bourbons, Albas, Centifolias, Damasks and Moss roses, which did not fit in at all with the formal bedding schemes of the Victorians. The flowers were wanted for the house, but the bushes did not fit the garden, so they were often separated out and grown on their own in walled kitchen gardens, along with the vegetables, for remember that we are talking about the mansions of the rich. The rose was still far from being an everyday plant.

It only became so quite gradually, in the early stages influenced by the fact that the rambler roses then coming into fashion could so easily be raised from cuttings by the workers on the big estates, and roses round their cottage doors became a reality. Then a little later there were the activities of an energetic band of clergymen led by the man who was to become Dean of Rochester, Reynolds Hole. Together, they formed The National Rose Society, as it was called in its early days and, together with several of the leading nurserymen, they wrote numerous books on growing roses which sold and sold. However, almost without exception they concentrated on growing roses for shows, for they were dedicated exhibitors themselves. Christian spirit or no, winning was the thing, and if you want to win you must cosset your roses, which means, of course, that they must be grown on their own so that they can be properly mulched, sprayed and generally groomed. Thus the idea that roses must be isolated in the garden was perpetuated and somehow the belief is still there in some people's minds.

Mind you, there is an argument for using Hybrid Teas and some Floribundas, with their generally rather stiff, upright growth, purely as bedding plants and keeping them to themselves. They are more difficult to blend in with other things, though it is not impossible. However, there are so many other kinds of roses of every conceivable size and shape that to say that they must all stand aloof is just plain nonsense.

There is another factor to take into account, too, for there will be, even with modern remontant varieties, at least six months of the year when the roses will be without either leaf or flower. With the old garden roses and the species the period without flowers will be even longer, though some of them do have attractive foliage to carry them through the balance of the summer and hips and even autumn colour later on. However, a great deal of old rose foliage is far from durable and can look extremely tatty towards the summer's end, making something to distract the eye from it very desirable. Mixing the roses with other shrubs is one answer, certainly for the bigger kinds, but the Gallicas and most Damasks will mix happily with ordinary border plants. However, it is not primarily with the old garden roses that we are concerned here. A little more about them will be said later on, but most of the roses dealt with in this book are very much more modern, are recurrent, and have comparatively attractive and durable foliage.

However, even then, as has been said, only about six months of the year are accounted for. Somehow we have come to accept a bed of pruned roses as a normal part of the garden scene, but why we have been prepared to put up with those ugly bare stumps and vast areas of bare earth for so long is a mystery. Even a ground-cover rose will shed its clothes in the winter.

There is, however, much we can do to bridge the gap, though perhaps not fill it completely. There are, after all, other parts of the garden equally bare and it is usually impossible to cater for them all.

However, before we get on to any kind of interplanting or underplanting it would be a good idea, as always, to try to see what others have done. Gardens where roses have been mixed with other plants in the most successful way include The National Trust garden of Sissinghurst Castle in Kent and, at the other end of the country, Newby Hall near Ripon in Yorkshire, and there are hundreds in between. Another National Trust garden, Polesden Lacey in Surrey has, for instance, no less than eight species or varieties of hardy geranium underplanting the roses and eleven kinds of hardy fuchsia interplanted among them, making a most effective combination.

The question as to whether one is going to use one of the persistent weedkillers such as simazene must also be gone into before any decision about mixed planting can be made. These are applied to the soil early in the season to prevent the germination of weed seeds, which saves a great deal of work later. However, if you do intend to use one you must abandon the idea of underplanting. Underplanting may also make mulching more difficult and, if the rosebed is a wide one, make it less easy to reach the roses for dead-heading, spraying and so on. However, as we know, the majority of the roses we are concerned with in this book are of the kind that spread out and cover a good deal of ground themselves. They will certainly smother some of the weeds, and in a small garden it is in any case rather more easy to keep on top of the weed problem than it would be in the rolling acres of a stately home. So it is probably best to say no to residual weedkillers in a small rose garden, but instead to plan things so that the roses and other plants take up every centimetre of soil and allow weeds no elbow room at all. This is not, surprising though it may seem, a very difficult thing to achieve, though it will take a year or two before all the plants join up and mingle satisfactorily. Meanwhile, you must weed and exercise patience, like the spring bulbs which have been waiting in the wings, ready for their introduction, for quite some time.

These are the things needed to cheer up the rather bleak prospect of bare rosebeds early in the year. The snowdrop (galanthus) hardly needs recommendation from me, but it is usually the first bulb in flower and multiplies itself prolifically once it is established. These and the other very early bulbs will not, of course, be companions to the roses, which will still be more or less dormant when they come out. That they will be substitutes, is even more of a pity with the next group of early bulbs, for most of them are blue. They include the scillas, grape hyacinths, chionodoxas and so on and would provide a colour that the roses lack. However, they are lovely on their own just the same. *Crocus tomasinianus* is another good plant for this time of year to brighten up the empty rosebeds, to be followed into bloom by species tulips. *Tulipa kaufmanniana*, white *T. turkestanica* and their hybrids will put on a brave show before the hyacinths arrive, which will be at the same time as the giant snowdrop, *Leucojum vernum*, fritillaries, and of course narcissus and daffodils in all their almost limitless variety. These will coincide with the first leaves appearing on the roses, their first stirrings into life after the long months of winter, and the ruby-red of so much of the early rose foliage looks particularly well with white narcissus.

Care must be taken not to plant the bulbs too close to the rose plants so that neither robs the other of soil nutrients, and the larger daffodils should certainly be positioned towards the back of the border. This is not just because they are the tallest, but because their leaves will be a long time in dying and can look very untidy long before they are due for removal in early June. Even the smaller plants like scillas make a lot of leaf growth after the flowers have faded, which should not be removed for some weeks to enable the bulbs to build up for the following season, and I suppose that, if meticulous tidiness in the garden is your passion, these early bulbs are best avoided. What a lot you would be missing, though.

Spring-flowering hellebores are another matter. Lovely in flower, both the green and the white kinds and the even more exotic purples of the *orientalis* hybrids will have, as their old foliage dies down (and is removed), new leaves pushing through which have a distinction all their own and last the summer through.

The late Brigadier Lucas-Philips, author of that enduring classic *The Small Garden*, recommended early-flowering dwarf rhododendrons and azaleas as companions for roses, and if they are of the evergreen kind I would certainly go along with that. However, rhododendrons do need an acid soil and thrive best in one that is not ideal for roses, so if you do try this combination you will probably not get the best out of either one or the other. If you do have rhododendron soil your roses will take much more looking after to give of their best, but that does not mean you should abandon all thought of growing them.

Moving from spring to summer, the range of possible plants to grow with roses becomes almost limitless, though among the best will be those with grey or grey-green leaves. A number of the hebes come into this category, among them *H. pageii*, which is one of the small-leaved, hardy ones. It needs renewing from cuttings every so often as it spreads and shows only bare stems in the middle after a while, but it makes a fine contrast to the roses and is a good plant for ground cover. Another good, grey-leaved plant, probably for edging more than anything else as it grows no more than 10–13cm (4–5in) tall, is *Anaphalis triplinervis*, which has long-lasting little powder-puffs of flowers. The grey-leaved varieties of rock rose will look well tumbling over the retaining walls of terraced beds in which miniature roses have been planted, but they do favour a dryish soil. Other possibilities are *Caryopteris clandonensis* for late blue flowers, catmint (bearing in mind that it tends to sprawl), verbascum, artemesias (particularly the shorter-growing *frigida* and *gnaphalodes*), the common culinary sage, rosemary, and perovskia in either its pink form or the violet *atriplicifolia*. The first of the two, at 60cm–1m (2–3ft) will be reasonably short but the latter may reach 1.5m (5ft) on good soil.

Stachys lanata might almost have been made of silver and many of the pinks and carnations, *Armeria maritima* and above all *Alchemilla mollis* are other recommendations, the latter having a soft, yellowish-green foliage rather than grey or silvery. It will need to be disciplined at regular intervals if it is not to establish its own dictatorship. There is a dwarf form, but it seems to be a rather wan little thing with none of the bounding energy of its bigger cousin.

One could go on listing plants like this for a very long time. For instance I have in my own garden a fine free-standing shrub of the pineapple broom, *Cytisus batandierii*, which has soft grey leaves and yellow flowers the shape of and smelling like pineapples. Into this I have grown 'Climbing Cécile Brunner', the small, pale pink flowers of which blend most happily with the silver leaves of the broom. In a small garden this combination might be too large to cope with, but *Cytisus batandierii* does make an excellent wall shrub. The question of combining these with roses has already been gone into in some detail in the chapter on climbing roses and so will not be pursued further here.

Hardy geraniums, already mentioned in connection with underplanting at Polesden Laccy, must get a brief airing before closing any list of plants for rosebeds. Varieties like *G. endressii*, *G. pratense* 'Johnson's Blue', *G.* 'Buxton's Variety', *G. macrorrhizum* and all the rest make wonderful carpeting plants, but most of them have to be watched or they will start climbing up and trying to smother the roses they are supposed to be complementing. However, they will take quite a drastic cutting back with a good grace and recover from it remarkably quickly.

We cannot leave the question of plants to grow with roses without considering the question of edging. In trying to assess what kind of plant to use some thought must be given to the kind of rose planting you are creating. If you are using the lax, informal type of rose such as 'Bonica' or 'Surrey', the informal approach to edging is best adopted and edging plants may not, in fact, be necessary at all. The roses themselves should be allowed to encroach a little on to the paths surrounding the rosebeds. However, with a more formal scheme, or an informal scheme where there are large gaps between the rose plantings, edging plants do very much come into their own. Box has been traditionally used and still takes a lot of beating, not least because its scent on a warm, humid day has a nostalgic, old-world appeal. Lavender is, however, my ideal plant for edging roses, and not only because it is relatively quick to establish. Its grey-green leaves and violet-purple flowers show off roses to perfection, though a certain amount of care must be exercised in making a choice of variety. Some make very big plants indeed, but *Lavendula spica* 'Hidcote' or 'Munstead Dwarf' will be quite suitable. Regular clipping over after flowering will help to keep them in good condition.

Some eyebrows may be raised when I suggest using heathers as edging plants for roses, and of course they come into the same category as rhododendrons. Rhododendron soil grows heathers and if that is what you have got, why not take advantage of it? They will be very suitable and blend very well, provided that you avoid those varieties with golden foliage for planting near the mauves and purples of many of the old garden roses. The winter-flowering kinds will, of course, help to relieve the bareness of rosebeds in the months from December to February or March.

SUPPLIERS AND SOCIETIES

Apuldrum Roses, Apuldrum Lane, Dell Quay, Chichester, West Sussex

David Austin Roses, Bowling Green Lane, Albrighton, Wolverhampton WV7 8EA

Peter Beales Roses, London Road, Attleborough, Norfolk NR17 1AY

Cants of Colchester, Ltd, Nyland Road, Colchester, Essex CO3 5UP

James Cocker & Sons, Whitemyers, Lang Stracht, Aberdeen AB9 2XH

Fryer's Nurseries, Ltd, Manchester Road, Knutsford, Cheshire WA16 0SX

Gandy's Roses, Ltd, North Kilworth, Lutterworth, Leics. LE17 6HZ

Gregory's Roses, The Rose Gardens, Stapleford, Nottingham NG9 7GA

R. Harkness & Co. Ltd, The Rose Gardens, Cambridge Road, Hitchin, Herts. SG4 0JT

Highfields Nurseries, Whitminster, Glos.

Hillier Nurseries (Winchester) Ltd, Ampfield House, Ampfield, Romsey, Hants. SO5 9PA

C. & K. Jones, Golden Fields Nurseries, Barrow Lane, Tarvin, Chester

E.B. Le Grice (Roses) Ltd, Norwich Road, North Walsham, Norfolk NR28 0DR

John Mattock Ltd, The Rose Nurseries, Nuneham Courtney, Oxford OX9 9PY

Notcutts Nurseries Ltd, Woodbridge, Suffolk IP12 4AF

Rosemary Roses, The Nurseries, Stapleford Lane, Toton, Beeston, Notts.

Stydd Nursery, Stonygate Lane, Ribchester, Preston, Lancs.

Warley Rose Gardens Ltd, Warley Street, Great Warley, Brentwood, Essex

A complete list of all roses for sale in the United Kingdom from nurserymen who are members of the Rose Growers' Association, and of which nurseries can supply the roses, is contained in *Find That Rose*, obtainable from Rose Growers' Association, 303 Mile End Road, Colchester, Essex CO4 5EA. A new edition appears each year.

Anyone interested in roses and rose growing should become a member of The Royal National Rose Society, whose address is Chiswell Green, St Albans, Herts. AL2 3NR.

GROWING IN THE UNITED STATES

America is a vast country with widely varying climates, from the sub-tropical in parts of the south to temperatures bordering on the arctic in the north. The difference is the equivalent of that between the northern countries of Europe and that of the Mediterranean region. It is this difference, and particularly the extreme cold that has to be met head on and dealt with, that makes the growing of roses in many parts of the United States more difficult than it is in the United Kingdom.

In the far south, the great heat and days of unbroken sunshine, coupled with the mildest of winters, means that the roses get little rest and may flower more or less continuously throughout the year if they are allowed to do so. There is no dormant resting period and, if this were not introduced artificially by quite hard pruning in the winter months, they would exhaust themselves and have to be replaced after a very few years. Watering, too, becomes of prime importance and gardeners may well have to consider some kind of permanent irrigation system, perhaps on a timer, at least during the hottest part of the year. A length of perforated hosepipe laid between the rose plants so that the water goes where it is needed—straight into the ground and not on to the blooms—is the easiest and best way of achieving this.

To back up the watering, mulching should be carried out, and in the USA there is a far wider range of suitable materials available, other than the usual forest bark and peatmoss (peat). Cacao hulls, ground corn cobs, buckwheat hulls, peanut shells and rice hulls are some of them.

Rose diseases and their treatment will not vary much from those described in Chapter 8, but among insect pests shoot and pith borers and, above all, the Japanese beetle are additions to the list. The effects of the latter can be devastating, but sprays suitable for dealing with chafers will help to control both the Japanese beetle and the other insects. The general rules for spraying apply and the control of gardening chemicals in both countries is very strict. Do not be tempted to experiment with any which have not been approved by the appropriate government agency.

What has been said so far involves relatively minor differences between growing roses in the United States and the United Kingdom. Far more radical measures need to be taken, however, when it comes to winter protection of the bushes in many central and northern states of America. Without these, the roses simply would not survive from one year to the next.

A great deal can be done with roses of all kinds to enable them to stand up to harsh conditions by looking after them properly. Well-grown, healthy plants and properly ripened wood as winter approaches will go a long way towards enabling them to survive where others less well cared for would perish. The hours of sunshine available for the ripening of the wood are very important, so do not plant your roses in a shady spot. At the same time properly sited screens of trees or shrubs can help by keeping away biting winds, which can often do a great deal of damage by dehydrating the plants.

The reason for winter protection is not so much to shield the roses from the cold itself as to keep them at a reasonably uniform temperature that is consistent with dormancy. Frozen ground is not the problem, but rapid changes of temperature may well be, freezing the sap in the canes one moment and thawing them out the next, breaking up the rose's cell structure.

Floribundas and hence their derivatives the patio roses, and in fact most of the modern small shrub roses described in this book, will usually get by in a temperature as low as –12° to –10°C (10–15°F) over a period of a week or two provided that loose soil is mounded up to a depth of about 30cm (12in) over the crown. Below 12°C (10°F) and something more is needed, especially in places where these low temperatures may go on for weeks, if not for months. For the roses that belong to families other than patio and modern shrubs, set out in the table are approximate temperatures below which full winter protection should be given. However, the figures should be taken only as a guide. As already explained, temperature alone is not the only factor. Wind chill can be just as calamitous. If in doubt, always err on the safe side.

Roses hardy to –20°C to –23°C (–5°F to –10°F)

Bourbons
Centifolias
China roses (including miniatures)
R. wichuraiana and its hybrids

Roses hardy to –23°C to –30°C (–10°F to –22°F)

Albas
Gallicas
R. pimpinellifolia and its hybrids

R. rugosa itself, the original species, is tougher still and will stand temperatures as low as –45°C (–50°F), but the same cannot be said for the modern hybrids such as 'Fimbriata' and 'Fru Dagmar Hastrup' which we grow in our gardens. Best to class them with the Albas and Gallicas as far as winter protection is concerned.

Here is the way of setting about giving your roses a safe passage through the winter, but before putting on any kind of protection there are a few things that must be done. All leaves remaining on the plants should be removed and all fallen leaves and the remains of mulches which could harbour disease cleared away. Soak the ground thoroughly with water and then carry on with your covering operations.

METHOD 1 involves mounding soil over the crown to a depth of 30cm (12in) and then leaving the rose exposed until the soil freezes. Then the entire mound should be covered with straw, kept in place with wire mesh. The straw will help to keep the soil frozen.

METHOD 2 involves covering the bush with a purpose-made polystyrene cone, held in place with a heavy stone and with soil mounded around the base to help to steady it.

METHOD 3 involves packing the bush with straw which is then wrapped in burlap and tied securely. Soil is then mounded around the base.

METHOD 4 involves surrounding the bush with a tarred paper cylinder and then filling the latter with bark or peat moss. Secure the top with burlap and once more mound soil around the base.

METHOD 5 Climbers can be brought through the winter by untying the canes from their supports, packing them with straw and then wrapping in burlap and mounding soil around the base.

METHOD 6 In extreme cases climbers and standards, and even bush roses, can have a trench dug, running away from one side of the rose. Dig up the roots on the other side, and lay the rose in the trench. Stems of standards and climbers should be held in place with pegs and then the whole rose covered in at least 10cm (4in) of soil.

Do not be in too much of a hurry to remove protective coverings the following year. Make sure as far as is possible that the cold spell really has ended and that the frost will not return. Otherwise the results could be disastrous.

18 Methods of winter protection

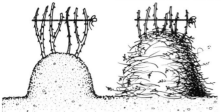

Mound soil at least 30 cm (12 inches) high over bud union of each bush (get soil from another part of garden); cover with straw after mounds freeze to keep mounds frozen.

Cylinder of wire mesh holds soil in place around canes, lets water drain away easily.

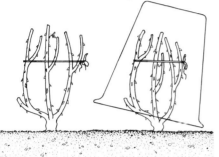

Styrofoam rose cones require tying of canes together, cutting them down to fit cones; brick on top and soil over flanges holds cones in place.

'Minnesota tip' for bush roses: dig roots on one side of bush, bend it over into trench, cover with soil.

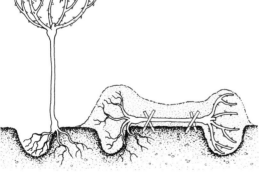

For 'tipping' standards, bend plant *over* bud union of roots and trunk, pin trunk to soil, cover.

Cold frame protects large bushes, hinged roof allows ventilation on warm days.

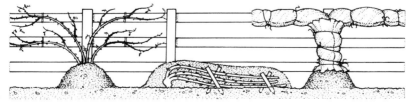

Protect climbers with soil mound where winter is 5°C–15°C; cover canes with soil if lows go below –10°C; insulate with straw wrapped in burlap for –10°C to 5°C.

Useful American rose nurseries

Armstrong Roses, P.O. Box 1089, Somis, Calif. 93066.

Antique Rose Emporium, Rt 5 Box 143, Brenham, Tex. 77833.

Carroll Gardens Inc., P.O. Box 310, 444 East Main Street, Westminster, Md. 21157.

Donovan's Roses, P.O. Box 37, 800, Shreveport, La. 71133-7800.

Heritage Rose Gardens, 40350 Wilderness Road, Branscomb, Calif. 95417.

High Country Rosarium, 1717 Downing Street at Park Avenue, Denver, Colo. 80218.

Inter-State Nurseries Inc., P.O. Box 208, Hamburg, Ia. 51640-0208.

Justice Miniature Roses, 5947 S.W. Kahle Road, Wilsonville, Oreg. 97070.

Kelly Brothers Nurseries Inc., Dansville, Ky. 14437.

Ligget's Rose Nursery, 1206 Curtiss Avenue, San Jose, Calif. 95125.

McDaniel's Miniature Roses, 7523 Zemco Street, Lemon Grove, Calif. 92045.

Mini-Roses, P.O. Box 245, Station A, Dallas, Tex. 75208.

Nor-East Miniature Roses, 58 Hammond Street, Rowley, Mass. 10969.

Roses by Fred Edmunds Inc., 6235 S.W. Kahle Road, Wilsonville, Oreg. 97070.

Roses of Yesterday and Today, 802 Brown's Valley Road, Watsonville, Calif. 95076.

Roseway Nurseries, Inc., 1567 Guild Road, P.O. Box 269, Woodland, Wash. 98674.

Sequoia Nursery, Moore Miniature Roses, 2519 East Noble Avenue, Visalia, Calif. 93277.

Wayside Gardens, Hodges, SC 29695-0001.

A complete list of roses on sale both in America and elsewhere, and where they may be purchased, is contained in *Combined Rose List*, issued yearly by Beverley R. Dobson, 215 Harriman Road, Irvington, NY 10533.

American rose growers should join the American Rose Society, P.O. Box 30, 000, Shreveport, La. 71130. Those especially interested in the old roses should also join one of the regional groups of The Heritage Rose Group. Details of the groups can be obtained from Charles A. Walker Jr, 1512 Gorman Street, Raleigh, NC 27606.

INDEX